The Civic Mission
of Museums

AMERICAN ALLIANCE OF MUSEUMS

The American Alliance of Museums (AAM) has been bringing museums together since 1906, helping to develop standards and best practices, gathering and sharing knowledge, and providing advocacy on issues of concern to the entire museum community. Representing more than 35,000 individual museum professionals and volunteers, institutions, and corporate partners serving the museum field, the Alliance stands for the broad scope of the museum community.

The American Alliance of Museums' mission is to champion museums and nurture excellence in partnership with its members and allies.

Books published by AAM further the Alliance's mission to make standards and best practices for the broad museum community widely available.

The Civic Mission
of Museums

Anthony Pennay

ROWMAN & LITTLEFIELD
Lanham • Boulder • New York • London

Published by Rowman & Littlefield
An imprint of The Rowman & Littlefield Publishing Group, Inc.
4501 Forbes Boulevard, Suite 200, Lanham, Maryland 20706
www.rowman.com

6 Tinworth Street, London SE11 5AL, United Kingdom

British Library Cataloguing in Publication Information Available

Library of Congress Cataloging-in-Publication Data

Names: Pennay, Anthony, author.
Title: The civic mission of museums / Anthony Pennay.
Description: Lanham : Rowman & Littlefield, 2020. | Series: American Alliance of Museums | Includes index. | Summary: "The Civic Mission of Museums, explores the way in which museums can leverage their collections and their connections within and beyond their communities to serve democracy as a whole"— Provided by publisher.
Identifiers: LCCN 2020037387 (print) | LCCN 2020037388 (ebook) | ISBN 9781538131848 (cloth) | ISBN 9781538131855 (paperback) | ISBN 9781538131862 (epub)
Subjects: LCSH: Museums—Educational aspects—United States. | Democracy and education—United States.
Classification: LCC AM7 .P46 2020 (print) | LCC AM7 (ebook) | DDC 069.07—dc23
LC record available at https://lccn.loc.gov/2020037387
LC ebook record available at https://lccn.loc.gov/2020037388

Contents

Acknowledgments

For Lia, Makaina, and Xander.
I have tried to work hard at work worth doing,
so that the world you inherit is worthy of you.

This book would not have been possible without the dedication, influence, and thoughtfulness of my family, friends, colleagues, and mentors. I have not written a book like this before. I am not an expert or a researcher. I am, at heart, a museum educator who enjoys gathering and sharing stories.

I am grateful to my grandparents, Richard and Louise Wilson, who first taught me the concept of citizenship, and then taught me about hard work. The best parts of who I am as a person can be traced directly to summers spent with them in Seeley Lake, Montana. This book is for you.

I am grateful to the remarkable teachers, professors, and professional mentors who have inspired me to be a lifelong learner. I am grateful for their passion, for their tough questions, and for all the times they pushed me to grow as a student, as a writer, and as a professional. Among them are Mick VanValkenburg, Nicholas Warner, Michael Riley, Ian MacMillan, Sia Figiel, Ted McConnell, Michelle Herczog, Kathleen Rowlands, and so many others. Whatever writing might be good here is thanks to your tremendous influence. Where it fails, well, I am still on the journey. This book is for you.

To the colleagues from across the field who've helped shape my (still-evolving) thinking as a museum educator and professional, and who've helped me learn my craft, I am grateful for your examples. To my EdCom and AAM colleagues—Nathan Richie, Hassan Najjar, Tim Rhue, Elissa Frankle, Kelly McKinley, Jason Porter, Megan Wood, Sheri Levinsky-Raskin, Dina Bailey, Mark Osterman, Monica Montgomery, Chris Taylor, Kyle Parsons,

Acknowledgments

Niki Stewart, Laura Lott, Julie Hart, Dean Phelus, Greg Stevens, Carol Stapp, Claudia Ocello, Veronica Alvarez, Sarah Jencks, and far too many to list properly—this book is for you.

Thanks also to my remarkable and amazing colleagues in the education department at the Ronald Reagan Presidential Foundation and Institute who dedicate themselves with full hearts and eager spirits to the cultivation of the next generation of citizen-leaders—Krista deKryger, Janet Tran, Rebekah Harding, Megan Gately, Erin Korsvall, Meredith Stasa, Colleen Hill, Tracey Sanders, Whitney Pagan, Ruben Lugo, Lori Love, and our entire team of inspiring educators both past and present. Though heart is never formally on any job description, the love and passion you bring to working with students and the public has inspired me for over a decade. Here's to "other duties as assigned." The long legacy of those other duties will be written in the deeds of the students we've served, and their contributions to the future. I am so incredibly proud to be part of Team EDU. This book is for you.

To the executive team and board of trustees at the foundation, who've supported, promoted, funded, and made possible our work in education, and whose generosity has impacted the lives of hundreds of thousands of students over the years, I extend many thanks. In particular, I owe a debt of gratitude to my supervisors during my time at the head of education—Joanne Drake and John Heubusch. Thank you for supporting our work and pushing me to grow. This book is for you.

To those I interviewed for this book, whether or not I specifically referenced the work at your museum, I appreciate your time and interest in this topic. Your thinking has been a powerful influence on the overall shape of this work—so thank you to Andrea Jones of Peak Experience Lab; Abby Pfisterer, Magdalena Mieri, and Christopher Wilson at the National Museum of American History; Brian Cofrancesco and Sally Whipple at Connecticut's Old State House; David Greenham from the Holocaust and Human Rights Center of Maine; Deborah Schwartz of the Brooklyn Historical Society; Elena Gonzalez; Kelley Szany of the Illinois Holocaust Museum and Education Center; Kristina Durocher of the Paul Creative Arts Center at the University of New Hampshire; Callie Hawkins of Lincoln's Cottage; Dr. Linda Blanshay at the Museum of Tolerance; Melonnie Hicks of the Pioneer City County Museum; Alecia Bryner of Morven Park; Jennifer Schantz and Samantha Rijkers of the New-York Historical Society; Pierce McManus and Anna Kassinger of the Newseum; and Shawn Lani of the Exploratorium. I hope I've done justice to the stories and work you shared with me.

I am grateful to Charles Harmon, my editor at Rowman & Littlefield, for his guidance and work to push me as a writer. Thank you for putting up with my flexible definition of deadlines.

I am grateful to my family and friends whose sage guidance and support has led me down this career pathway, including my friends of several decades: Steve and Debbie, Steve and Mary, Derek, and Peter—your friendship has helped make me who I am. Thanks also to Chris and Cynthia, my family by choice; to my mom, Cheryl, who has supported and celebrated me in ways only a mother could; to my father, Bob, and stepmom, Beth, who have been there for me through thick and thin; and to my brother, Chris, his wife, Jen, and my new nephew, Hunter. To my sister, Jessica, I hope to help build a world that we'll both be proud of. This book is for every one of you.

Finally, to my children, Lia, Makaina, and Xander—I'd like to do my part to leave this all better for you. I love you, and this book is for you.

Preface

Working hard for something we don't care about is called stress. Working hard for something we love is called passion.

—Simon Sinek

If you don't like something, change it. If you can't change it, change your attitude.

—Maya Angelou

In 2010, after teaching middle school history and language arts for a decade, I took my career steering wheel, signaled a lane change, and made the shift from the world of classroom education to the world of museum education. It was a palpable change. On Friday, I left a vibrant classroom of middle school students with an armload of handmade cards and pictures, eager to begin my new life as program manager. I arrived on Monday at my museum, met my supervisor, and took the elevator to the lower level where my cubicle awaited me.

My role had not existed before at my museum. You see, after receiving a major grant to develop civic learning programs and curriculum, the museum was able to hire three staff members. We had a mission statement, which included the following, "Our aim is to develop proactive, informed, educated, and conscientious citizens and leaders." We had some wonderful, thoughtful, brilliant colleagues with great minds, good intentions, and a fervent desire to help build a better democracy. Other than that, we had a giant blank slate. For the first time in my career as an educator, there was not a classroom of students, a textbook to help drive instruction, or a set of state-mandated curriculum items to cover.

While we felt confident in our ability to develop programs and curriculum, we weren't entirely sure about what it meant to be in the profession of citizen cultivation. We decided to do some research. In 2003, the Carnegie Corporation and CIRCLE (Center for Information and Research on Civic Learning and Engagement at Tufts University) published a report entitled *The Civic Mission of Schools.* The report made recommendations for some best practices to promote civic learning in America's schools. In 2011, a follow-up report called *Guardian of Democracy: The Civic Mission of Schools* was published, and, after a decade of declining instruction in history and social studies, it cited an urgent need for civic learning. Democracy itself, it argued, was in danger. Then came the election of 2016, which, some would argue, was one of the most divisive and destructive elections in the history of the country. The patient was sick, and everyone could see it. Following the election, I received emails from nearly every professional organization with which I associate—national, state, and local museum, history, social studies, and civic learning groups—whose message was, "Our work is more important now than it has ever been."

Despite the title of the report, *The Civic Mission of Schools*, the responsibility to help cultivate thoughtful, engaged, and informed citizens is not confined to the formal P–12 education system. Indeed, museums and other informal learning institutions are uniquely positioned to play a critical role in promoting the civic health of their communities and this nation. For many years, the field has focused on visitor engagement and experience, on making a connection between an institution and the community it serves. This book will make the argument that the product of that connection—the outcome of that engagement with visitors—should result in a positive civic benefit.

A number of books published in recent years deal with museums making connections with their audiences and communities, for example, Nina Simon's *The Participatory Museum* and *The Art of Relevance,* or Anne Bergeron and Beth Tuttle's *Magnetic: The Art and Science of Engagement.* Other books might be very specifically focused on pedagogical techniques within a museum, for example, *Museum Gallery Activities: A Handbook* by Sharon Vatsky, or on how one might manage their career as a museum educator, like Leah Melber's *Teaching the Museum: Careers in Museum Education.* In some ways, *The Civic Mission of Museums* will bring these various strands together—connecting with audiences and community for a very specific civic purpose; pedagogical techniques that promote civic knowledge, virtue, and engagement; and professional development that leads museum educators and frontline staff toward connecting their work to the broader task of citizen building.

This book is primarily intended for those who work directly with the public—those participating in education teams, providing visitor services, directing curatorial or interpretative programs, or interacting with the community in any other capacity. Senior staff, executive directors, and board members might also consider the importance of embracing a civic mission throughout the work of their institution.

Since the days of John Cotton Dana, museums have sought to maintain relevance in the daily lives of their communities. Over the past several decades, museums have shifted, as a field, from focusing on collections to connecting with visitors, diverse audiences, and their community. *The Civic Mission of Museums* explores the ways in which museums can leverage their collections and their connections within and beyond their communities to serve democracy as a whole. What role do museums play in cultivating the next generation of citizens? How can museums serve as laboratories of democracy? And, in times of growing divisions across our country, how can museums build the bridges that ensure progress toward "a more perfect union"? This book will explore the historic civic mission of museums, examine case studies where a diverse range of museums tackle the work of building a better democracy, and offer tips for any museum to better fulfill its civic mission.

WHAT THIS BOOK IS

This book will ground itself in the context of the past, first giving a high-level overview of the long history of the connection between education and democracy, briefly exploring the ebb and flow of American civic engagement, and then zooming in on the present state of affairs. This will include a focus on the work of Robert Putnam, who describes the gradual decline of civic institutions in America. Next, it will explore the history of museums, and the evolution of both the role of educator and the work of the museum. I will call on the writings and thinking of John Cotton Dana, Elaine Heumann Gurian, and others with regard to the evolving civic mission of museums. History will establish a framework, presenting museums as an essential civic space. Then, in light of the shifts in museums, culture, politics, et cetera that have occurred over the past few decades, I will look to examples of the roles museums are beginning to embrace as civic hubs and as civic actors, while exploring what the future of museums might look like in terms of civic action and engagement. I will share a number of case studies from a broad spectrum of museums—diverse in geography, size, institutional focus, mission, and outcomes. In examining these case studies, I will draw on scholarship connected to civic learning as a whole.

As such, I frame the case studies through a spectrum of interconnected pieces of civic learning. I start by defining and sharing examples of how museums collect, share, curate, and collaborate around *civic knowledge*. Next, I explore the work museums do to cultivate the mental habits of engaged citizens through a chapter on *civic mindset*. Then, we contrast the work of an art museum, a science museum, and a presidential library, in exploring how museums can foster essential *civic skillsets*. We move on to how museums can work with their communities to take *civic action*. Finally, I use the metaphor of a garden to share a *civic toolkit* that any institution, regardless of size, focus, or budget, can draw on as it sets about its own civic work.

WHAT THIS BOOK IS NOT

My undergraduate degree is in literature and film studies. My master's is in English, with a focus on creative writing. I have always been interested in stories. As such, this work attempts to tell a broad story of what civic work in museums looks like. I am not an academic or a researcher, so I don't anticipate this will read like a scholarly work. It is not a particularly comprehensive work. The stories I share in the book are based on conversations I had with museum professionals from across the country, articles and books I've read, and programs I have seen firsthand. To explore, comprehensively, the civic work of museums writ large would take several lifetimes. In 2014, the Institute of Museum and Library Services estimated that there were 35,144 museums in the United States. The museums represented in this work represent an incredibly small fraction of that number. As such, the work described here is just the very tip of the iceberg in terms of what is being done across the country. Instead of a political statement arguing for one element of civic learning over another, it is more about the interconnectedness between knowledge, mindset, skillset, and action. And it is definitely not a didactic work that will instruct museums on how best to do civic work. Rather I hope it serves to stoke conversations and thinking through examples and conclusions.

As opposed to a "be-all, end-all" statement on the civic work of museums, this is, I hope, a contribution to the ongoing and evolving conversation about what museums can do to produce a benefit for the communities in which they exist.

THE CONTENT

In developing the content for this book, I conducted a series of interviews with museum professionals from across the country. I know some of them personally and had seen or heard about their work firsthand. Some reached out to me, when I posted about this project in various online forums, wanting to share what their institutions are doing. As a member of various civic learning communities, much of my background knowledge comes from attending gatherings and conferences over the course of the past decade. Serving on various volunteer boards and advisory committees, such as the EdCom Professional Network for the American Alliance of Museums and the California K–12 Civic Learning Task Force, as well as participating in the CivXNow Coalition and others, has also given me valuable insights.

MY HOPE

Civic learning is incredibly important to me, for all sorts of reasons. Though I am not a historian, I am a lover of history. I avidly consume the history of the presidency, of politics, of ideas, of art, of science, of the progress and regress of humankind. Without a basic knowledge of history, we live in a disconnected present. And even though we are, through technology, more connected than ever, we are drifting ever farther apart. History, the story of what we've done and where we've been, is a set of roots that holds us together. I believe in the power of museums to teach, to preserve, to bring people together, to inspire, and to celebrate the very best of what humans can achieve. I am, by nature, an optimist who believes in the power of people and institutions to do what is right over time. Even as people in our country drift farther apart politically and civically, even as we increasingly lose faith in civic institutions, like in any drought or storm, I believe we'll make it through to the other side and be better for it. And I believe that museums will be essential to weathering the storm. My final reason for why this topic is important to me is deeply personal. I have three kids. I want them to grow up in a community, a country, and a world that exemplifies the best of what is possible so that, one day, they'll be able to stand on the shoulders of our generation and reach farther, achieve more, and get along better than we've been able to do. And they'll do it, in part, because our museums have been able to tell the right stories, inspire and foster the right thinking, and compel the sorts of actions that drive us onward and upward.

1

The Civic Mission of Museums

*[A] good museum is a proper and **helpful institution to any community**
which may establish and maintain the same.*

—John Cotton Dana, The New Museum (1917)

*The commitment to education as central to museum's **public service** must
be clearly expressed in every museum's mission and pivotal to every museum's activities.*

*Assert that museums place education—in the broadest sense of the word
at the center of their public service role. Assure that the **commitment to
serve the public** is clearly stated in every museum's mission and central to
every museum's activities.* (emphasis mine)

—*Excellence and Equity*, American Association of Museums (1992)

The word **civic** originates from the Latin term *corona civica* or "civic
crown." At the height of the Roman Republic, a republic which prided itself
on its military prowess, the *corona civica* served as one of the highest honors
a citizen could receive. Comprised of the interwoven leaves of an oak, this
natural, simple crown took on a significance beyond its humble construction.
Citizens who earned the crown could wear the leaves to public events for the
duration of their lives. According to Pliny, even the lofty members of the Senate would rise, pay their respects, and invite the bearer of the *corona civica* to
sit beside them. In addition to the public adulation, "he himself and his father
and his paternal grandfather [were] exempt from all public duties."[1]

Augustus, first emperor of the Roman Empire, earned the *corona civica*
for bringing an end to the civil wars that followed the assassination of Cae-
sar. The relative peace that followed, known as the Pax Romana, lasted for

1

Figure 1.1. Augustus, emperor of the Roman Empire, depicted wearing the *corona civica*
Bibi Saint-Pol, Palace Bevilacqua, Verona

more than two hundred years as the Roman Empire extended its territory and increased its population to roughly seventy million people, one-third of the world's population at the time.

Augustus is often depicted in art wearing the *corona civica*. For what it is worth, Augustus chose to root his title in his role as a citizen as well, eschewing any number of possible traditional monarch titles in favor of *princeps civitatis* or "first citizen of the state."

Modern definitions of **civic** are broad. As an adjective, *Merriam-Webster* defines civic as "of or relating to a citizen, a city, citizenship, or community affairs."[2] Civic duty, civic pride, and civic leaders are offered as examples of how the word might be properly used.

Alternatively, the Urban Dictionary, a crowdsourced slang reference website, whose motto is "Define Your World," has seventy different definitions of **civic**, sixty-nine of which center around various insults about, hot takes on, or heated defenses of the Honda that bears the name. The fourth most popular definition, as decided by user votes, is typical:

1. a japanese economy car
2. a car that teenager's rich parents buy them as a cheap reliable transportation, but then they [f*#$] it all up by putting huge fart cans and spoilers on them trying to drive fast and race everyone and thinking they are really cool but everyone is really just laughing at them because they are so goddamn stupid.[3]

The sole exception to this lively debate shows up as the eighth definition. On the second page, hidden among the sprawling back and forth on Hondas, we find a definition that deals with the public dimension of the word "civic." The definition offered by user "Joe the Student" differs substantially from the lofty Latin origins.

civics
Possibly the most useless class that kids today are forced to take. Learn about the government and about issues no one cares about.[4]

For the purpose of this book, I embrace these varied definitions. On one hand, the civic mission of museums is deeply rooted in history, and in a centuries-long connection between education and democracy. Thomas Jefferson not only wrote the Declaration of Independence and served as the third president, he founded the University of Virginia. Ben Franklin, who attended the Constitutional Convention as its oldest and most revered (save for only George Washington) citizen, also founded the University of Pennsylvania. In fact, when the founders emerged from Independence Hall in Philadelphia after months of secretive deliberation as they forged the Constitution, a woman in the crowd famously asked, "Doctor, what have we got? A republic or a monarchy?" Dr. Franklin's reply?

"A republic, if you can keep it."

Are museums up to the task of keeping the republic? If so, what does it mean to be a keeper? On the other hand, the civic mission of museums will be flushed out in more modern terms as well.

of or relating to a citizen, a city, citizenship, or community affairs

I also choose to embrace the sense of the word "citizen" that dates back to roughly 1300, "inhabitant of a city or town,"[5] rather than the more politically charged and legal interpretation so often cited today. How we **relate** to those who live in our cities and communities is an essential part of how museums fulfill their civic mission.

This book will be about all of this. It will be about the noble and historically grounded civic mission of museums. It will be about the ways in which museums preserve and pass along and interpret the long history of the world. It will be about statues and urns and art and history and context and objects. It will be about the many ways museums collect, store, and share **civic knowledge**.

But it won't **just** be about knowledge. In Latin, there is a difference between the words *educare* and *educere*. Both *educare* and *educere* are infinitive forms—conjugated in the first-person singular present indicative as *educo*—so they have the same etymological bloodlines, if you will. That said, there is an important difference. *Educare* means to "bring up, to train, to teach."[6] This definition more closely aligns with the medieval through industrial learning model. Standing in front of a room, a learned teacher, professor, or educator shares the fruits of a lifetime of intense study, reflection, and thought with a room full of empty vessels waiting to be filled. These eager students and learners take copious notes, ask earnest questions, and dutifully do their best to learn from the master.

In college, one of my favorite professors employed this model. He entered the classroom after every student had taken a seat. He walked past us without speaking. He dropped his bag on a chair at the front of the room and removed a yellow pad whose dog-eared pages were filled from edge to edge with his indecipherable scribbles. Then, for an hour or so, he lectured from his notes, occasionally made a connection in his mind to another strand of thought, excitedly wandered from one side of the class to the other, his hands dramatically waving back and forth to make his points. With a few minutes left, he silently and solemnly gazed at the final scribble on his notepad, decided he had concluded, and asked if there were any questions. There being none, he gathered his belongings, and exited the room. This was *educare*. He would teach. We would, in theory, and if our aching hands could take notes fast enough, learn.

Educere, on the other hand, has an entirely different approach. It means "to lead, draw, take out, forth, away."[7] A local high school we partner with on many projects has the Latin motto *Audet Ducere*, or "dares to lead." This definition of education has everything to do with leadership. Here, education is not based in receiving information or training, it is a bold action. It requires a degree of bravery and audacity from both the leader and those who are led. In recent years, the difference between these two styles of educating has been popularized with a clever rhyme. It's a shift from "Sage on the Stage" to "Guide on the Side." *Educere* is not just receiving information from someone who knows more; rather it is concerned with creating meaning. It means the guide or educator values the contributions of the learner. It suggests that learning itself is a productive act that involves far more than accumulating knowledge.

Contrast the story of my professor above with a learning experience I had while studying abroad in Sydney, Australia. I signed up for the archaeology class because, quite frankly, I wanted to be Indiana Jones. When I went to the bookstore to pick up my materials for class, I was quite surprised to find a series of heavy textbooks instead of a fedora, a whip, and a leather jacket. *This is not the archaeology I was promised by Spielberg.* Though we had plenty of *educare* lectures, I still have vivid recollections of the day we went on an archaeological dig. Rather than simply telling me about the work of archaeologists, and showing me pictures in a textbook or a presentation of what professionals had discovered, the professor took us to an archaeological lab, briefly demonstrated some basic techniques, and allowed each of us to explore samples from a shell midden that had been brought back from a dig.

I went in with the expectation that, in digging through these samples, I would most certainly be the student to uncover a priceless artifact— probably a gold- or diamond-encrusted goblet with curious and supernatural powers. After spending the better part of thirty minutes carefully digging and brushing through my sample, I uncovered no such object. The professor must have seen the frustration on my face. She came over.

"What did you find?"

"Nothing really. Some broken shells. A few little rocks. Lots of dirt."

"Nothing?" She asked. "Not quite."

She then proceeded to point out the evidence that was right before me. The shells indicated the types of food the aboriginals consumed, which, in turn, showed evidence of the sorts of fishing techniques they employed. The rocks were not just rocks, she explained. They were used as tools. She picked one up and demonstrated, then handed it to me and encouraged me to use the tool in a similar fashion. I don't quite know how to explain what happened next, but it's almost as if my 2D understanding of life suddenly popped and became 3D. This isn't to say I became an expert, but she was able to connect me to an object and lead me through a process of understanding the significance a little better. While I can't remember the subject or any of the content from my *educare* lecture, I vividly recall, more than twenty years later, the afternoon I spent in the *educere* archaeology lab.

However, this book will not just be about the sharing of **civic knowledge** that is often associated with museums and learning. Civic learning is about far more than the acquisition of knowledge. Effective citizens, those who value contributing to a better community, don't just gather and store knowledge. They have to also learn how to apply the knowledge of the past to the present. Beyond knowledge, we must ask ourselves: How do museums contribute to a **civic mindset, skillset, and action?**[8]

That is, how can museums help cultivate the mental habits of engaged and informed citizens? What does it mean to wrestle with policy, with tough history, with current events? How do we tackle challenging community issues?

In examining civic mindset, we'll explore the ways in which museums promote, teach, foster, and provide a space for the development of certain mental habits that contribute to engaged and informed citizenship including:

- Self-Awareness
- Self-Management
- Self-Efficacy/Agency
- Social Awareness
- Political Awareness
- Political Efficacy (belief that one's civic or political actions make a difference)
- Tolerance
- Empathy
- Creating/Defining Community Values[9]

Also, it will be about how museums contribute to a **civic skillset**. As we investigate the work museums are doing to develop civic skillsets, we'll look specifically at how museums are working with those in their communities to improve civic skills such as:

- Communication Skills
- Interpersonal Skills

- Democratic Simulations
- Communication around Controversial/Political Issues
- Gathering and Analyzing Data on Civic Matters/Issues
- Making Informed Decisions/Taking Informed Action[10]

Finally, we'll explore the ways in which museums promote, encourage, and serve as a catalyst for **civic action**—which, in theory, is the logical output of civic knowledge, mindset, and skillset. If a community has the knowledge, the mental habits, and the skills necessary to effect positive change, it takes civic action. So we'll also explore the ways in which museums promote, teach, foster, and provide a space for the following:

- Deliberative Discussion
- Exploring Historic and Current Events
- Volunteering
- Hosting and Attending Public Meetings
- Voting Opportunities
- Service Learning/Community Service
- Recognizing or Awarding Civic Action[11]

Taken as a whole, this book suggests that museums can best fulfill their civic mission when they:

1. Share civic knowledge
2. Foster civic mindset
3. Cultivate civic skillsets
4. Serve as a catalyst for productive civic action

The following pages will explore the many ways in which museums do this important work.

CONTEXT FOR ME

The first museum I ever loved was the Metropolitan Museum of Art (the Met) in New York City. I loved it despite not seeing it in person until well after college. My parents divorced when I was four. My mom, who had custody of my brother and me (and later my sister), didn't make much money. Travel meant a trip to visit our grandparents. So, most of my youthful adventures took place only in my head and as a result of the vivid imagery of whatever author happened to cross my way. Unlike many children who find an author or genre to their liking, and stick with it, I was a generalist. If the book had a cover and pages, I'd read it. I loved history, adventure, science fiction, fantasy, mystery—you name it. So long as I could escape the four walls of my room and mentally meander through the worlds of my host protagonists, I welcomed any avenue of escape.

One Christmas, my grandmother bought me a collection of Newbery Medal–winning books—five cheap paperbacks shoved together with a cardboard cover and wrapped in cellophane. I ripped it open and E. L. Konigsburg's 1967 award winner, *From the Mixed-Up Files of Mrs. Basil E. Frankweiler*, tumbled out. I shoved the other four into the overflowing corners of my bookshelf and dove into the world of Claudia and Jamie Kincaid. For those who haven't read the book, Claudia and Jamie run away from home and decide they are going to live at the Metropolitan Museum of Art. They take money from the fountain, buy food from the vending machines, mix in with touring school groups, and sleep in an antique bed gifted to the Met by Irwin Untermyer. In the course of the narrative, they become fascinated by a new exhibit—a statue of an angel. The sculptor is unknown, but many suspect it is a previously unknown Michelangelo. The children are fascinated by the story, conduct their own research, and submit their findings to the team at the Met anonymously.

It had everything my fanciful ten-year-old brain could handle. History, adventure, mystery, empowered children solving a riddle that professional adults couldn't. Sneaking around a museum at night, decades before *Night at the Museum*, sounded like the life. Inspired by Claudia and Jamie, I decided to run away myself and live in a museum. I emptied my piggy bank, threw a jacket over my pajamas, waited until my mother fell asleep, opened the window of my room, removed the screen, slipped out into the backyard, and scaled the wooden fence that separated my safe home from the vast world. I, too, was going to live in a museum.

I made it to the stop sign at the end of the street, a whole four houses away, before I decided that the darkness between the streetlights was far too ominous to continue. Not to mention, I couldn't be sure if I needed to turn right or left to reach the Met. Oh yeah, and I grew up in San Jose, California—on the other side of the country. I ran back to the fence, replaced the screen, closed the window, and curled up in my bed. It was another two decades before I found myself spending most of my waking hours in a museum.

In college I majored in literature and film studies. Mostly, I liked stories and wanted to tell them. My grandmother suggested I should read all the stories I wanted, but maybe take a business class or two.

"Don't you want a job when you graduate?" she asked.

Turns out, a passion for narrative isn't too lucrative. I applied for several positions, including a management trainee job at an industrial supply company, selling server space to startup tech companies, working for the state park system, at a wilderness program meant to serve as an alternative to incarceration for teenagers, and with Teach for America. Rejected by all but Teach for America, I began teaching language arts in Southern California, inspired by the vision that "One day all children in this nation will have the opportunity to attain an excellent education."

On my first day at Woodrow Wilson Middle School in Pasadena, California, I got a visceral preview of the challenges ahead when I went to pick up my supplies for the year. I arrived at the supply closet, and the administrator there handed me a single ball-point pen and a single sharpened pencil, wrapped together with a rubber band.

"Here you go," she said.

I laughed. They were just messing with the newbie. It took me about fifteen seconds to realize there were no more supplies coming my way.

"Oh, you're serious?"

She nodded.

I loved my students there, but, in retrospect, I was not a great teacher. I dutifully used the textbooks and copied the appropriate handouts and chapter quizzes. Professional development consisted largely of a fifteen-minute tutorial on how to use the teacher's edition of the textbook. I spent a lot of time preaching the value of education, how education created opportunities, and telling my students that there were no limits to what they could achieve. But, unfortunately for my students, I was far more *educare* than *educere* in my approach. After two years of teaching, I decided to go back to school.

I studied creative writing at the University of Hawaii, and, under the influence of a visiting author and poet from Samoa, Sia Figiel, I fell in love with the genre of magical realism. I imagined I'd be a writer, creating the sorts of fantastical worlds I'd loved as a kid. I published a few short stories online. I presented a story at a writer's conference called "The Ballad of Blueberry Joe" where the protagonist, as punishment for drawing guns on his spelling test at school, was planted in the woods and slowly turned into a tree. I received an award for a short story about coin divers off the coast of Catalina Island. I wrote a novel for my master's thesis and submitted it to every publisher and agent I could find. I received a few polite rejection letters, but mostly my contribution to the world canon of great literature was met with no response at all. After two years of teaching, and two years in grad school, my grandmother asked me the same question.

"Don't you want a job when you graduate?"

So, with no agent or publisher interested in my abilities as a writer, I went back to the classroom. This time it was at a private religious day school on the west side of Los Angeles. It was a small school, and if I wanted the job, I had to teach history as well as English. I had never taught history before, but I liked eating, so I accepted the job and said I could do it. In contrast to my first day in Pasadena, the administrator at the private school handed me a supply catalog.

"Order what you need," she said.

"Do I have a budget?" I asked.

"Order what you need."

Again, I stood there for fifteen seconds or so before I realized she was serious.

My first year of teaching history was abysmal. My students hated it. I hated it. On Friday afternoon, we sat there hating it together until school was out for the week. I used the textbook and often I was only a day or two ahead of my students. In California, the state standards dictate that seventh grade world history spans a thousand years and six continents. As you can imagine, there is not a lot of depth, but there are a whole lot of facts. Picture the excitement of my seventh-grade students when I would stand before them with the textbook open to the appropriate page.

"Today we will learn seventeen facts. This includes six key terms from this chapter, five key people, and of course, six dates that you must absolutely, positively remember."

The lone bright spot of the year, instructionally, came when we took a trip to the Skirball Cultural Center, a museum about fifteen minutes from the school. We participated in a hands-on archaeological dig that brought me flashbacks to my powerful learning experience in Australia. A week later, I pitched a complete revamp of my history curriculum to my principal.

I told her, "I want it to be like a museum. Hands on. Interactive. Alive."

She agreed and I spent the summer trying to turn my seventh grade history course into a museum. Instead of chapters from the textbook, we examined primary sources, conducted archaeological digs, researched and interpreted historic figures from the Renaissance, and curated our own classroom museum with objects we created when looking through the online collections of museums around the world. Students wrote their own label copy, explaining the significance of their object in the broader context of what we were learning. We blogged about our findings, and shared them with the world at large. The highlight of my second year came when, at the end of a simulation of the signing of the Magna Carta, the bell rang indicating the end of class.

Figure 1.2. The Skirball Cultural Center in Los Angeles, California
Photo by Hughwa

"Mr. Pennay," said one of the students. "Can we please have more social studies?" From there, it was only a matter of time until I found myself full time in a museum.

Five years later, I had shifted nearly completely to experiential learning in my classroom. I had even moved to a charter school focused solely on project-based learning. While there, I signed up to attend a professional development session for teachers being held at the Ronald Reagan Presidential Library. The education director at the time, Krista Kohlhausen, had been recently hired to start up a new education division. She shared her vision for the future of their education work, and mentioned they were looking for someone with a passion for history, civic learning, and technology who wanted to work with a national audience of teachers and students. I sent in my resume that night.

CONTEXT FOR THE FIELD

The predecessors of modern museums were collections, typically compiled by a wealthy patron, meant to inspire awe, but also to showcase the wealth, sophistication, and learnedness of the collector. From the Medici's Uffizi Gallery in Florence, Italy (begun in 1560, opened to the public in 1765, and becoming a museum in 1865) to Archduke Ferdinand of Austria's *Kunstkammer* or "cabinet of art and marvels," which also dates back to the mid-1500s, museums originated around collections. They existed, to use part of the great Stephen Weil phrase, because they were concerned with "being about **something**."

Often that *something* meant a curious mixture of the power of the object itself; the skill and craftsmanship of its creator; the taste, intellect, and stature of its collector; and the collective reverence and power of those whose status merited the opportunity to appreciate said objects. Before the Ferrari existed, there were museums. One could argue, that the museum itself, the collection, existed as an alternate version of the *corona civica*. Rather than a laurel of oak leaves publicly signifying their virtue as citizens, these early founders of museums gathered the works of the leading thinkers, artists, scientists, and shared the wonders and curiosities. The more outstanding the collection, the more outstanding the collector. Who needs a crown of leaves when you have a collection of the Renaissance masters?

Over time though, this **something** has evolved, and museums have evolved as well. No longer is the purpose of museums as a whole to simply serve as a nice repository for important cultural, political, artistic, and historical artifacts.

In his 1917 classic work of museology, *The New Museum*, John Cotton Dana wrote, "The essentials of museum existence—a home, collections properly so called, an income and, **most important of all these essentials, such activities as may fairly be supposed to produce beneficial effects on their respective communities**"[12] (emphasis mine). Here Dana posits two essential ideas for the broad civic mission of museums.

First, museums are not just collections; they are also places that should **produce** a positive effect on their communities. The word "produce" here is critical. To produce something means to take an active role in bringing it into existence. Farmers toil in the fields to **produce** crops. An artist spends years learning her craft to **produce** something beautiful, complex, and challenging. A construction worker sweats and strains to **produce** a public building. In thinking, and writing, and interviewing, a writer works to **produce** a book. Dana does not say "to have a beneficial effect," because "have" is passive. To merely state that a museum "should have" a positive effect says nothing about the active choice to create that effect. "Produce" signals that museums must be proactive in bringing about "beneficial effects in their respective communities."

Elaine Heumann Gurian develops this idea in the introduction to her 2006 collection of essays, *Civilizing the Museum*. She writes, "No society can remain civil without providing places where strangers can safely associate together. I have called such civic places—which include museums—'congregant spaces.'"[13] Gurian's congregant spaces, then, are one of the beneficial effects underlying the existence of a museum. In order to benefit their communities, museums serve as gathering spaces, places where the affairs of the community can be explored as a community.

The second critical aspect of this description by John Cotton Dana is when he states, "most important of all these essentials." Not only should museums produce positive effects for their communities, it is the most important reason for their existence. By Dana's definition, collections exist, and are important, but only in the sense that they serve the more essential purpose of positive public benefit. If the earlier versions of museums replace the *corona civica* as larger, flashier, more learned symbols of civic engagement and success, the Dana version of museums is more concerned with the substance than the style. In Dana's vision, the museum, like the bearer of the crown of antiquity, is the civic hero.

Fast forward to 1973. A rabble-rousing group of educators in attendance at the annual meeting of the American Association of Museums (AAM) (later the American Alliance of Museums) forged a professional network, EdCom, devoted to the work of education in museums. In an oral history given at the 2013 EdCom luncheon at the AAM Annual Meeting, one of the founders, Bonnie Pittman, described a museum culture from the early seventies that placed an emphasis on collections and those who tended them. In describing the climate for museum educators at the time, she said, "It was a very difficult time, and we were not recognized. We all lived in the basement of our museums. . . . Then the curators were gods, and when we said we want to be gods with you, they said, 'No.'"[14] Those who worked with children, those who worked to forge connections between museums, their collections, and their visitors, often felt powerless.

However, Pittman implied, whether they believed it or not, they had power. In describing the importance of the work of museum education staff, she reminded the audience that tax exempt status for museums is a result of the education work that museums do. Education and public service are inextricably linked. For decades, centuries even, this meant the *educare* version of education. The visitor served as an empty vessel, a pail ready to be filled with the knowledge of the collection's learned caretaker. The educator served merely as a ladle, a means to an end.

Pittman, who would go on to chair the AAM Task Force on Museum Education in 1989, led the creation of the landmark report *Excellence and Equity* edited by Ellen Cochran Hirzy. The first of three key ideas espoused in the report is "the commitment to education as central to museum's public service must be clearly expressed in every museum's mission and pivotal to every museum's activities."[15] *Excellence and Equity* picks up on Dana's idea that public service is the most essential element of a museum's mission. Just as Dana redefined the museum as an institution focused on producing a public benefit, *Excellence and Equity* "speaks to a new definition of museums as institutions of public service and education, a term that includes exploration, study observation, critical thinking, contemplation, and dialogue. Museums perform their most fruitful public service by providing an educational experience in the broadest sense."[16] Here, the work of the museum educator shifts from *educare* to *educere*—instead of being the ladle working to fill the empty vessel, the museum educator, like the museum, is an intersection. Here, the content, the mission, the visitor, the community, and the world at large collide. It is the job of the museum educator to help construct meaning—"to lead, draw or take out, forth or away." Given a constantly evolving mixture of audience, context, history, and the world, the educator must *produce* something for someone. This is a civic act. And it is powerful.

Education then, is not, as is often the misperception, merely the domain of those folks in the basement who work with the kids. Rather, *Excellence and Equity* is based on an expanded notion of public service and education as a museum-wide endeavor that involves trustee, staff, and volunteer values and attitudes; exhibitions; public and school programs; publications; public relations efforts; research; decisions about the physical environment of the museum; and choices about collecting and preserving."[17] Museum education is not just teachers working with the students. It is the museum, as an institution, at every level working with its community, as a group of citizens, at every level, to produce a positive effect for the community. In doing so, it is adhering to the modern interpretation of the word civic. A museum performs its *civic duty* when working with and helping cultivate *civic leaders.* Here, regardless of title or function, the entire institution works to fulfill its civic and education mission.

The word "civic" itself is also about power. In a 2012 essay for *The Atlantic*, Eric Liu, founder of Citizen University and keynote speaker at the 2014 EdCom Luncheon, wrote "Why Civics Class Should be Sexy." In it he proposed "to revive civics by making it squarely about the thing people are too often afraid to talk about in schools: *power*, and the ways it is won and wielded in a democracy. Imagine a curriculum that taught students how to be powerful—not only to *feel* empowered but to be fluent in the language of power and facile in its exercise."[18]

There are countless museums across the country whose collections, subjects, or namesakes address these very questions. Historic homes, presidential libraries, historical societies, art museums, cultural centers are often centered in stories of power. Who won power? Who lost power? How did they wield the power they had? In telling these stories, in choosing how to tell them, who to include, and how to engage the community in their telling, museums have tremendous power themselves.

AAM explored the public service role of museums further in 2002 with the publication of *Mastering Civic Engagement: A Challenge to Museums.* Ellen Hirzy wrote,

> Civic engagement occurs when museum and community intersect—in subtle and overt ways, over time, and as an accepted and natural way of doing business. The museum becomes a center where people gather to meet and converse, a place that celebrates the richness of individual and collective experience, and a participant in collaborative problem solving. It is an active visible player in civic life, a safe haven, and a trusted incubator of change. These are among the possibilities inherent in each museum's own definition and expression of community.[19]

Like Gurian, Hirzy highlights the role of museum as a community gathering space. Gurian calls the museum a "congregant space," and Hirzy points out that this space, the museum, serves as an intersection. This collaboration between institution and community is what causes the civic engagement that is so important to the work of a museum.

It is also important to note the use of the word "trust" here. In order to have that positive community benefit so essential to Dana, to wield that civic power, the civic work must be rooted in a trusted institution. In the early 2000s and beyond, it has not been easy to find such a place, as trust in most public institutions had been dropping across the board for decades. Gallup has been tracking public confidence in various institutions since the seventies. Table 1.1 shows the high and low points of public confidence in various institutions.[20]

Bucking this trend, however, are museums. Despite a steady pattern of the public losing faith in institutions as a whole (the institutions cited in table 1.1

Table 1.1. Loss of Trust in American Institutions Over Time

Institution	People Who Have a Great Deal or Quite a Lot of Confidence: High Point	People Who Have a Great Deal or Quite a Lot of Confidence: Low Point	Net Change
Newspapers	51% (1979)	22% (2007)	−29%
Public Schools	62% (1975)	26% (2014)	−36%
Congress	42% (1973)	7% (2014)	−35%
Banks	60% (1979)	21% (2012)	−39%
Big Business	34% (1975)	16% (2009)	−18%
Church	68% (1975)	38% (2018)	−30%

lost an average of roughly 31 percent of public confidence over the course of thirty plus years), museums are trusted by the public at an incredibly high level. As Ellen Hirzy noted in *Mastering Civic Engagement*,

> Museums have substantial potential as civic enterprises that contribute to building and sustaining community, and they are ready to pursue this potential. As stewards and as educators, museums are dedicated to excellence, they are respected as unsurpassed sources of intellectual capital, the objects and ideas that are the raw material of the museum experience. They also are respected for the exceptional ways in which they share their intellectual capital with the public, as educators and as sources of inspiration and wonder. **Museums engender great confidence, and Americans trust them wholeheartedly as objective resources.**[21]

She cites a 2001 study, commissioned by AAM that showed 87 percent of Americans find museums to be trustworthy.

As one of the very few groups of institutions that are trusted by Americans, museums have power. It is a tremendous power. It is groups of citizens in our communities placing their faith in our work and our institution. To trust means to feel safe in the presence of a museum, to feel as though the museum and those who represent the institution are good-faith actors who have the interests of the community in mind. To be trusted is to be infused with tremendous power.

Gurian wrote, "All humans have history and should have access to it. Museums are part of a set of institutions that house such histories, or 'institutions of memory.'"[22] In choosing what stories to tell, how to tell those stories, and who is included or excluded from the telling, museums wield that tremendous power.

What does Spiderman teach us about power?

With great power comes great responsibility.

The civic mission of museums, then, is primarily concerned with how we choose to exercise that power, and how we work to fulfill that responsibility to our communities.

CONTEXT FOR THE WORLD

By many indicators, democracy, as we know it in the United States, is in decline. Each year since 2006, *The Economist* has published a study called the *Democracy Index*. According the 2018 version of this study, the United States is rated as a "flawed democracy." Over the course of the past ten years, the United States has fallen from a ranking of eighteenth place in 2008, to twenty-fifth place by 2018. "This primarily reflects a deterioration in the functioning of government category, as political polarisation has become more pronounced and public confidence in institutions has weakened. . . . The highly partisan nature of Washington politics is contributing to this trend, as parties are increasingly seen as being focused on blocking one another's agenda, to the detriment of policymaking."[23] This is in stark contrast to our neighbors to the north, Canada, who rank sixth in the world and have never been outside the top ten.

In 2014, the Pew Research Center shared data that showed that "Republicans and Democrats are more divided along ideological lines—and partisan antipathy is deeper and more extensive—than at any point in the last two decades."[24] Not only has the percentage of people who hold consistently partisan opinions more than doubled in the past twenty years, the average Democrat has shifted to the Left as the average Republican has shifted to the Right. Astonishingly, according to the study, "92% of Republicans are to the right of the median Democrat, and 94% of Democrats are to the left of the median Republican." What does this sort of political shift mean? It means that as we drift further away in terms of ideology from one another, resentment and anger build. In 1994, 16 percent of Democrats had a "very unfavorable" attitude toward Republicans, and 17 percent of Republicans felt the same about Democrats. Twenty years later, 38 percent of Democrats feel "very unfavorable" toward Republicans, and more than one-quarter—27 percent—view the Republican Party "as a threat to the nation's well-being." On the other side of the aisle, 43 percent of Republicans view Democrats "very unfavorable" with 36 percent seeing Democrats as a threat to the nation.

As a nation, we are losing faith in institutions, losing faith in those who believe differently than we do, and sorting ourselves, both online and in our communities, into increasingly homogeneous groups. At the same time, as we surround ourselves with those who think like us, we withdraw from civic participation.

In his oft-cited bestseller, *Bowling Alone: The Collapse and Revival of American Community*, Robert Putnam describes the decline in participation in community organizations. Citing a steady decline in civic participation that dates back to the 1960s, he writes,

> most Americans no longer spend much time in community organizations—we've stopped doing committee work, stopped serving as officers, and stopped going to meetings. And all this despite rapid increases in education that have given more of us than ever before the skills, the resources, and the interests that once fostered civic engagement. In short, Americans have been dropping out in droves, not merely from political life, but from organized community life more generally.[25]

Since the publication of *Bowling Alone*, we've experienced nearly another two decades of rapid change in communication, information, the media, and society in general with the growth of the internet and smartphones.

In an essay for *Mastering Civic Engagement*, Chris Gates, former president of the National Civic League, drew on Putnam's work when he pointed out another period of rapid change—the nineteenth century. Rapid changes in media, finance, and transportation produced a profound shift in American life then too. Gates writes, "These changes reduced the connections between people, made old forms of collective problem solving obsolete, and forced the country to invent new ways of building what Putnam calls bridging and bonding social capital—i.e., developing relationships of trust and reciprocity both with those who are like us (bonding) and those who are different from us (bridging)."[26] Gates goes on to cite the litany of civic and professional organizations that came into being a decade or two before and after the turn of the century. Between 1880 and 1920, organizations such as the Salvation Army, Red Cross, Goodwill, Rotary, Lions Club, League of Women Voters, and the American Association of Museums all came into existence.

According to Putnam, we've been withdrawing from these sorts of associations and organizations at a steady clip for roughly half a century. Looking at the Pew data tells us that, in the current state of affairs, we are doing a fairly good job of creating the bonding social capital. Through social media algorithms, and news and media sources that cater to and confirm political and ideological biases, we are bonded with those who are similar like never before. In a 2012 study by Ron Johnston, David Manley, and Kelvyn Jones in *Annals of the American Association of Geographers,* the study found "that polarization increased by 29 percent across Census regions, 12 percent across states, and 14 percent across counties"[27] between 1992 and 2012.

What we aren't doing so well is the bridging. Therein lies the opportunity for museums. Gates continues,

Museums are vital institutions for preserving memory, sustaining culture, and creating identity. This trinity—memory, culture, and identity—is essential to the moral and psychological development of individuals, communities, and societies . . . museums help equip us to understand each other and ourselves. And it is this understanding that animates our efforts to strengthen democracy, promote civic engagement, and build community.[28]

Museums do not exist absent the context of the world around us. We have a challenge ahead of us. We live in a world where there is partisan rancor, a toxic political environment, and a nation slowly and steadily withdrawing from civic life, and a general lack of faith that political institutions can even tackle these issues without arguing amongst themselves in fundraising circles over and over again. The good news? Museums are more than ready to meet this challenge. They have evolved for more than a century preparing for exactly this moment. We're right where we are meant to be.

We are the keepers we need.

NOTES

1. Pliny. 1952. *Pliny: Natural History, Volume IX, Books 33–35*. Translated by H. Rackam. Cambridge: Harvard University Press.

2. "Civic." n.d. Retrieved March 14, 2019, from https://www.merriam-webster.com/dictionary/civic.

3. "Civic." April 12, 2003. Retrieved March 14, 2019, from https://www.urban dictionary.com/define.php?term=Civic.

4. "Civics." March 4, 2009. Retrieved March 15, 2019, from https://www.urban dictionary.com/define.php?term=Civic.

5. "Citizen (n.)." n.d. Retrieved March 15, 2019, from https://www.etymonline.com/word/citizen.

6. "Educare." n.d. Retrieved March 15, 2019, from https://en.wiktionary.org/wiki/educare#Latin.

7. "Educere." n.d. Retrieved March 15, 2019, from https://en.wiktionary.org/wiki/educere.

8. In examining these, I will draw on the work of the Center for Educational Equity at Teachers College, Columbia University, who compiled research summaries on "Civic Knowledge and Cognitive Skills;" "Values, Dispositions, and Attitudes;" and "Political and Civic Behavior" for the Civic Learning Impact and Measurement Convening, hosted by the CivXNow Coalition in 2019.

9. Center for Educational Equity, Teachers College, Columbia University. 2018. Research Summary: "Values, Dispositions and Attitudes, December 2018." Retrieved from https://portal.civxnow.org/sites/default/files/resources/Research%20Summary-Values%20Dispositions%20and%20Attitudes%2012-13-18.pdf.

10. Center for Educational Equity. 2018. "Values, Dispositions and Attitudes."

11. Center for Educational Equity, Teachers College, Columbia University. 2018. Research Summary: "Political and Civic Behavior, December 2018." Retrieved from https://www.civxnow.org/sites/default/files/basic_page/Research%20Summary-Political%20and%20Civic%20Behavior%2012-13-18.pdf.

12. Dana, J. C. 1917. *The New Museum*. Woodstock, VT: Elm Tree Press.

13. Gurian, E. H. 2007. *Civilizing the Museum: The Collected Writings of Elaine Heumann Gurian*. London: Routledge.

14. "Looking Back/Looking Forward: EdCom at 40." May 23, 2013. Retrieved from https://www.youtube.com/watch?v=2L0wEz128-I.

15. American Association of Museums (AAM). 1992. *Excellence and Equity: Education and the Public Dimension of Museums*. Washington, D.C.

16. AAM. 1992. *Excellence and Equity*.

17. AAM. 1992. *Excellence and Equity*.

18. Liu, E. 2012. "Why Civics Class Should Be Sexy." *Atlantic*, April 13, 2012. Retrieved from https://www.theatlantic.com/national/archive/2012/04/why-civics-class-should-be-sexy/255858/.

19. American Association of Museums (AAM). 2002. *Mastering Civic Engagement: A Challenge to Museums*. Washington, DC.

20. Gallup. 2019. "Confidence in Institutions." November 11, 2019. Retrieved February 25, 2020, from https://news.gallup.com/poll/1597/confidence-institutions.aspx

21. AAM. 2002. *Mastering Civic Engagement.*

22. Gurian. 2007. *Civilizing the Museum.*

23. Economist Intelligence Unit. 2018. *Democracy Index 2018: Me too? Political Participation, Protest, and Democracy.* New York: Economist Intelligence Unit.

24. Pew Research Center. 2019. "Political Polarization in the American Public." December 31, 2019. Retrieved from https://www.people-press.org/2014/06/12/political-polarization-in-the-american-public/.

25. Putnam, R. D. 2001. *Bowling Alone: The Collapse and Revival of American Community.* New York: Simon & Schuster.

26. AAM. 2002. *Mastering Civic Engagement.*

27. Florida, R. 2016. "America's 'Big Sort' Is Only Getting Bigger." Bloomberg CityLab and University of Toronto's School of Cities and Rotman School of Management. October 25, 2016. Retrieved from https://www.citylab.com/equity/2016/10/the-big-sort-revisited/504830/.

28. AAM. 2002. *Mastering Civic Engagement.*

2

Civic Knowledge in/and Museums

Knowledge is power. Information is liberating. Education is the premise of progress, in every society, in every family.

—Kofi Annan, United Nations Secretary General (1997)

Shall I teach you about knowledge? What you know, you know, what you don't know, you don't know. This is true wisdom.

—Confucius

On February 1, 1960, David Richmond, Franklin McCain, Ezell Blair Jr., and Joseph McNeil, four freshmen at North Carolina Agricultural and Technical College, in a protest against segregation, sat down at the counter of a Woolworth's in Greensboro, North Carolina, and quietly ordered a cup of coffee. Though they were denied service at the "whites only" counter, the young African American men refused to leave their seats, choosing instead to sit patiently until the store closed. They returned to campus, shared their story, and encouraged others to join them the next day.

On February 2, 1960, the four returned, this time with more than twenty Black students in total. They took seats at the counter, asked to be served, and were again refused. The students kept occupied with schoolwork and stayed seated at the counter for several hours. They were harassed by many of the white customers. A local TV news crew and the police showed up.

On February 3, 1960, the four returned. At this point, more than sixty students had joined the sit-ins. White customers showed up to threaten, intimidate, harass, and yell at the students. In addition to the news and the police, the Ku Klux Klan showed up. The students, still denied service, did their best to quietly read and study.

On February 4, several hundred protesters showed up. By the end of March, the protests had spread to more than fifty cities over thirteen states. By the end of July, the store had lost hundreds of thousands of dollars in revenue as a result of the protests, and they finally agreed to integrate their lunch counter. They asked several of their Black employees to take a seat, and, in serving them, brought the protests to an end.

The protest of the Greensboro Four inspired many across the South and across the country. Five years after the Montgomery, Alabama, bus boycotts inspired by the courage of Rosa Parks, and three years before Martin Luther King Jr.'s iconic "I Have a Dream" speech in Washington, DC, they weren't the first or the only protests during the civil rights movement. Certainly, by any objective standard, these sits-ins, and their immediate and long-term impacts, should be included on a list of essential pieces of civic knowledge. They represent a crucial moment in the civil rights movement. A movement, which, in many ways traces the entire arc of the history of the United States and is a defining theme of our shared history. In this chapter, we'll look to define civic knowledge; to better understand the national, state, and local factors influencing what sorts of civic knowledge are passed from one generation to the next; and, once determined, to examine how museums and the country assess whether or not the civic knowledge that is most essential has been learned.

WHAT IS CIVIC KNOWLEDGE?

We explored the meaning and the historic roots of the word civic in the first chapter. Here, being clear both on what *knowledge* means, as well as how it interacts with the civic piece, is essential to better understanding how museums approach civic knowledge. The Center for Education Equity at Teachers College, Columbia University says, "Civic knowledge starts with an understanding of the structure of government and the processes of lawmaking and policy-making, but a broader, deeper knowledge of history, politics, economics, and other disciplines is necessary to comprehend the wide range of issues that citizens face."[1] **Civic knowledge** then is the facts, information, and skills members of a community acquire that inform their understanding of and participation in their communities. Museums, writ large, address the issues that citizens face in a wide variety of ways via different types of institutions. What follows is a few illustrative, but by no means comprehensive, examples:

- **Key Events or Movements:** The National Center for Civil and Human Rights in Atlanta, the Birmingham Civil Rights Institute in Alabama, the National World War I Museum and Memorial in Kansas City, the National World War II Museum in New Orleans, the National Constitution Center in Philadelphia, and the United States Holocaust Memorial Museum in Washington, DC
- **People:** presidential libraries, the King Center in Atlanta, the Harriet Tubman Underground Railroad Visitor Center in Maryland, and many monuments across the country
- **Places:** national parks, Mount Vernon, historic homes and sites
- **Information:** Library of Congress, the National Archives, and local and regional libraries and archives
- **Skills:** As we'll see in a few chapters, many of the various museums, zoos, aquariums, etc. throughout the country have programs, exhibits, or training that leverage the civic skills of the past to shape and inform the civic skills of the present.

Civic knowledge sometimes celebrates the most outstanding exemplars, leaders, and heroes of our past. Sometimes museums lay bare the horrors and pain caused by the very worst of our history. Civic knowledge is all these things.

The National Council for the Social Studies (NCSS), described as "the largest professional association for social studies educators in the world,"[2] frames knowledge as part of a broader societal necessity. In the introduction to the National Curriculum Standards for the Social Studies, NCSS writes, "The aim of social studies is the promotion of civic competence—the knowledge, intellectual processes, and democratic dispositions required of students to be active and engaged participants in public life."[3]

By this definition, and as this book will explore, civic knowledge is an essential and constituent part of a much broader civic framework, a combination of knowledge, skills, and action. NCSS labels it "civic competence." Elaine Heumann Gurian writes that "all humans have history and should have access to it"[4] and labels museums "institutions of memory." Museums, and their learning cousins such as schools, libraries, and archives, then, are like the Brothers Grimm, who collected their stories, or "The Giver" in Lois Lowry's Newbery Medal–winning book of the same name, charged with keeping the memories of a civilization. You cannot build the skills you need as a citizen, or thoughtfully take civic action, without a baseline of shared civic knowledge.

In their National Curriculum Standards, NCSS argues that "young people who are knowledgeable, skillful, and committed to democracy are necessary to sustaining and improving our democratic way of life." So, in order to be a contributing citizen, one whose efforts sustain and improve our national political way of life, one must exhibit a degree of civic competence—in this case a blend of historical and political knowledge, skills, and a commitment to democracy. If we were planting a garden of democracy, knowledge would serve as the soil—necessary, full of nutrients, possessing the ability to sustain and help cultivate engaged and informed citizens. If we establish knowledge as the baseline of a museum's civic mission, several questions arise.

What is it, in fact, that we should know? Are there levels of knowledge? Some documents, events, objects, or facts might be essential pieces of civic knowledge. Some might be merely good to know. Some might be wonderful to know *if* one has the time and energy to pursue learning about them. Once it is determined which pieces of knowledge must be learned, how do we go about teaching that knowledge or curating an exhibit that tells the story of that object, place, or time? How do we frame the information in such a way that it is accessible to the public, and to the wide range of students, adults, and visitors who might, by choice or by requirement, be exposed to that information? And then, how do we assess the impact or the "stickiness factor" or the relevance of that information?

GOALS

In the state of California, where I live and work, the standards for civic knowledge are set at the state level by the California State Board of Education. Though the standards are adopted by the state board, they are "not binding on local educational agencies or other entities. Except for the statutes, regulations, and court decisions that are referenced herein, the document is exemplary, and compliance with it is not mandatory."[5] Museums are also not bound in any way to these standards, but they certainly take them into account for the purposes of education programming.

At the national level, there is similar deference on what constitutes essential civic knowledge. In the 2010 revision to their National Curriculum Standards, NCSS writes, "These revised standards do not represent a set of mandated outcomes or an attempt to establish a national social studies curriculum. The United States Constitution left the responsibility for education to the individual states, and although there are federal guidelines and mandates, the specific social studies requirements, the specific scope-and-sequence, and the frequency and nature of social studies assessments vary from state to state."[6]

California is the largest state in the country in terms of population. It serves more than six million students through more than 11,500 public and charter schools each year.[7] In fact, it has more students enrolled than the smallest twenty states combined, and at least double the number of students of every single state except for Texas.[8] This power in numbers means a lot of influence. In the classroom it means that California standards play a significant role in the design of textbooks nationwide. For museums, it means that many of us are aligning or, at the very least, attempting to connect, our interpretation, curriculum design, and/or education programs to those standards as well.

The "Core Standards for Museums" set forth by the American Alliance of Museums (AAM) says that a museum must assert "its public service role and [place] education at the center of that role."[9] With such a wide range of institutional focus, including art, history, children's museums, zoos, aquariums, botanical gardens, cultural centers, and more, it is nearly impossible to require any sort of specific civic knowledge of museums writ large. Museums, then, play a critical role in helping define what civic knowledge should be. If a museum includes an object in an exhibition, the story of a person or group of people in its narrative, or focuses on an event or a set of changes, it is, by default, saying to its audience that by including this in the work of our museum, we elevate this content or idea or program to the level of essential civic knowledge. Where it makes sense to do so, they often also connect this content to local, state, or national school learning standards. So, though museums are not, in any way, bound by state or national education standards, they often proudly promote the ways in which their collections and education materials fulfill those standards.

COLLECTIONS AND CONNECTIONS

A cursory visit of the web pages of the Los Angeles County Museum of Art, the Ronald Reagan Presidential Library, the Natural History Museum of Los Angeles County, the J. Paul Getty Museum, the USS Midway Museum, the San Diego Museum of Man (now the Museum of Us), the Exploratorium, the San Francisco Museum of Modern Art, and many other museums throughout the state indicates content that aligns with or explicates the California state standards.

As a former classroom teacher, regardless of the process museums used to connect to the standards, I appreciated this tremendously. In the first chapter, I briefly shared the story of how a trip to the Skirball Cultural Center changed the way I taught in the classroom. It is because they articulated a case for how their content directly connected to the state standards that I was able to make such a case.

The standards for grade seven demand that "after reviewing the ancient world and the ways in which archaeologists and historians uncover the past, students study the history and geography of great civilizations that were developing concurrently throughout the world during medieval and early modern times."[10] What better way for students to review the ways in which archaeologists help uncover and tell the stories of the past than for students to become archaeologists and tell the story of the past?

Prior to my integration of this activity, my class spent a week learning all the relevant definitions, looking at photographs of archaeologists in the field, listening to audio and video of archaeologists talking about their work, and answering questions on a test. However, the students really "got" it when they *experienced* the work of an archaeologist. It reminds me of a saying about the power of experiential learning:

> *Tell me, and I will listen;*
> *Teach me, and I'll remember;*
> *Involve me, and I will learn.*

Through the power of a museum experience, my students really learned about what it meant to be an archaeologist, and in ways that are not necessarily easy to assess.

The one national measure we have for measuring civic knowledge is the National Assessment of Educational Progress (NAEP), also known as the Nation's Report Card. The NAEP for Civics is "designed to measure the civics knowledge and skills that are critical to the responsibilities of citizenship in the constitutional democracy of the United States."[11] The NAEP makes no distinction about where the civics knowledge comes from, so for students taking the test, the knowledge they are drawing from will be based on each individual student's memory and experience. For any student, that combination might consist of school learning, museum learning, books, websites, video games, and any other source that might serve as an input for knowledge. So how are we doing?

Results from the 2010 NAEP indicated that "fewer than half of American eighth graders knew the purpose of the Bill of Rights,"[12] despite the fact that the purpose is in the title. In 2014, only 23 percent of our nation's eighth grade students were classified as "proficient" in civic knowledge, though 74 percent were classified as having a basic proficiency.[13] However, the emphasis on literacy and math ushered in by the No Child Left Behind assessment policies that have driven assessment nationally means that many have labeled the lack of civic content a "crisis." A simple Google search of "civic education crisis" returns a blog post from David Davenport at Stanford University's Hoover Institution titled "The Civic Education Crisis." He argues that "by almost any measure, the quality of civic education in America has become a national crisis."[14] A 2016 report by the American Council of Trustees and Alumni (ACTA) had a similarly frightening title, *A Crisis in Civic Education.* In the report, ACTA writes, "There is a crisis in American civic education.

Survey after survey shows that recent college graduates are alarmingly igno-rant of America's history and heritage. They cannot identify the term lengths of members of Congress, the substance of the First Amendment, or the origin of the separation of powers. They do not know the Father of the Constitution, and nearly 10% say that Judith Sheindlin— 'Judge Judy'—is on the Supreme Court."[15] If there is such a crisis, how can and should museums respond? How can museums, which safeguard, interpret, collect, and share the stories, arti-facts, and events of our collective past, best contribute to solving this crisis?

There are many institutions that already fully embrace the civic mission of museums. In a 2006 article in *Prologue*, the quarterly publication of the Na-tional Archives and Records Administration (NARA), Ninth Archivist of the United States Allen Weinstein writes, "The mission of 'civic education' is now embedded in NARA's new Strategic Plan. One of our five goals now reads: 'We will increase civic literacy in America through our museum, public outreach, and education programs.'"[16] The National Archives has quite a reach. Accord-ing to their 2018 Annual Report, the archives served 1,214,601 museum visitors in person, and another 1.32 million visitors to their docsteach.org website.[17] The number of visitors exceeds the number of students in public schools in thirty-eight states and the District of Columbia.[18]

Several museums, in response to this crisis, have joined a relatively new coalition of organizations working to solve the problem of a lack of qual-ity civic learning in our nation. Housed through iCivics, the civics-based video game nonprofit founded by former Supreme Court Justice Sandra Day O'Connor, this group is called the CivXNow Coalition. On their website, in explaining their mission, CivXNow cites a 2018 study led by the "George W. Bush Institute in collaboration with the Penn Biden Center for Diplomacy and Global Engagement and Freedom House found that–even in our polarized nation–89% of Americans agree that we need more civic education."[19] The CivXNow Coalition is a network of nonprofits, programmers, funders, mu-seums, libraries, and organizations who "pledge to ensure that every young person acquires the civic knowledge, skills, and behaviors necessary for informed and authentic civic engagement." Of the nearly one hundred organi-zations of all types that have joined the coalition, there are several museums. These include the Edward M. Kennedy Institute for the United States Senate, the John F. Kennedy Library Foundation, the National Archives Foundation, the National Constitution Center, the Newseum (which has since closed; the parent organization, Freedom Forum, is still in operation), and my employer, the Ronald Reagan Presidential Foundation and Institute.

These institutions represent just a small percentage of the museums that embrace a civic mission at the core of what they do, and that collect and share essential civic knowledge across a multitude of programs, resources, exhibits, and curriculum.

In fact, museums as a whole spend more than $2 billion[20] each year on education activities, which exceeds what the US Department of Education grants to every state except for California, which received just over $2 billion[21] from the federal government. According to AAM, museums also "receive approximately 55 million visits each year from students in school groups."[22] The National Center for Education Statistics expected that in the fall of 2020, student enrollment in public elementary and secondary schools would reach fifty-one million. Let that sink in for just a moment. Museums, as a whole, serve more students than the entire public school system of the United States.

It goes without saying that museums often approach learning in a much different way than do schools, and it isn't fair to consider these numbers as an apples-to-apples comparison. This data is merely used to illustrate a larger point. Museums collectively wield tremendous financial resources, hold incredible cultural capital, and possess the power to influence millions of students and visitors each year.

With this background on how civic knowledge is defined, shared, and assessed, we will return to the Greensboro sit-ins, and this landmark moment in American history.

CIVIC KNOWLEDGE AND LAYERS OF CONTEXT

In *Civilizing the Museum*, Elaine Heumann Gurian writes, "Museums are social-service providers . . . because they are spaces belonging to the citizenry at large, expounding on ideas that inform and stir the population to contemplate and occasionally to act. . . . We need museums and their siblings because we need collective history set in congregant locations in order to remain civilized. Societies build these institutions because they authenticate the social contract. They are collective evidence that we were here."[23]

Gurian suggests that the civic knowledge being shared through our institutions should inform, inspire contemplation, and occasionally inspire action. Earlier in this chapter we explored the idea of civic knowledge serving as the soil for how museums approach our civic and public service mission. Knowledge is power. It is the root of any effective building of skills or action. However, as any gardener knows, there isn't just one type of soil. There are benefits and limitations of clay soil, sandy soil, silt soils, and sometimes mixes of soils designed to help gardeners create the perfect garden. The same is true of civic knowledge. What civic knowledge looks like will vary depending on the context, community, and goals of the institution sharing the civic knowledge. The questions that are essential for museums then are: What do we hold, preserve, collect, and share as essential civic knowledge? Why? How do we distribute and share the civic knowledge?

Let's go back to the Greensboro Woolworth's counter. In 1960 it was the setting for one of the most powerful, inspiring, and compelling episodes of the civil rights movement, making national headlines and inspiring further protests across the country. In 1993, the same counter represented something else—the end of an era.

In 1979, Woolworth's celebrated its one-hundredth anniversary and had become the largest department store chain in the world with more than eight hundred shops. Its five-and-dime model served as inspiration for today's dollar stores. Its lunch counters, some argue, are the predecessors of the modern mall food courts. But less than fifteen years after its peak, in October 1993, with the growth of retail and big-box stores like Walmart, Best Buy, Target, and others, Woolworth's was breathing its last corporate breath.

In a 1996 article for the Smithsonian online publication *increase & diffusion*, William Yeingst, now curator emeritus of the Smithsonian National Museum of American History (NMAH), described his reaction while listening to the business report on the local news and learning that the F. W. Woolworth Corporation was planning to shut down hundreds of stores across the country. "The immediate question that flashed into my mind was whether the Elm Street store in Greensboro, North Carolina was included in the corporate restructuring. Was the luncheonette intact after thirty-three years?"[24]

Yeingst then called and spoke to the manager of the Greensboro store, who confirmed that it would be among those closing. Yeingst, in a behind-the-scenes interview with objectofhistory.org, said he contacted Woolworth's corporate vice president for public relations about acquiring the counter for the Smithsonian. "I tried to make the point that this was an object of national significance, regional significance, but also local significance to the community of Greensboro."[25]

In his contemplation of the significance of the Greensboro Woolworth's counter as an object, Yeingst also suggests a framework for museums and civic knowledge in general. The Greensboro lunch counter presents a powerful example because the counter as an object, as a physical piece of civic knowledge, plays a prominent role in four different museums, illustrating civic knowledge in terms of national, regional, local, and, to add to Mr. Yeingst's framework, experiential significance.

NATIONAL SIGNIFICANCE

In her 1992 essay "The Importance of 'And,'" Elaine Heumann Gurian writes, "We can simultaneously be citizens of the country, even the world, and be functioning members of our specific community."[26] This is true. As citizens, we inhabit a multitude of communities. We are civic actors in our homes, at our places of work or school, in our cities, our counties, our states, our regions, our nation, and the world. We are connected to news, events, and people across these various communities through the wonders of the modern networked world. In the early days of our country, news of events would spread only as fast as the quickest horse or boat might carry it. For example, news of the Declaration of Independence took more than a month to spread from the colonies in America across the Atlantic. First published in Pennsylvanian news outlets on July 2 and 3, 1776, the news of the American declaration was not carried in the British news until August 10, a full five weeks later.

Today, something can happen in the far corners of the world and be live-streamed over the internet as it happens. If a tragedy happens in France, people all over the world can update their Facebook profile picture with a French flag filter within minutes to show solidarity or support. With pop-up news feeds, instant online reactions, and hot takes in abundance across a litany of platforms, the average person can be inspired, outraged, stirred to action, and made to feel helpless all within the span of a twenty-four-hour news cycle. By the time the next week rolls around, those items that so inspired and outraged just the previous week have often been forgotten, or seem like events from the distant past.

With so much knowledge and content being created daily, how do museums select which items deserve to be elevated to the level of essential civic knowledge? Yeingst knew the moment he heard the report of the Woolworth's

Figure 2.1.   Exterior of the F. W. Woolworth store, site of the Greensboro sit-ins, an essential piece of American civic knowledge
Photo by dbking

closing that the counter was an essential piece of American history and shared civic knowledge and should be included in the broad story of America being told at NMAH. It is a story that encapsulates civic knowledge. It is, all at once, a story of history, of policy-making, of economics, of government writ large, and of the power of the individual citizen. It is a story of what happened in the past, but also an example of how citizens can affect change today.

Gurian writes that "government[s], large and small, build museums to celebrate their achievements," and that the "citizen visitor's motivation for seeing these museums leans more to patriotic pilgrimage that ordinary museum-going."[27] The National Museum of American History is one of nineteen museums and galleries that comprise the Smithsonian Institution, the largest "museum, education and research complex" in the world. The Smithsonian receives $1 billion[28] in funding from the federal government. "The Institution, established in 1846, is governed by a board of regents which, by law, is composed of the vice president of the United States, the chief justice of the United States, three members of the Senate, three members of the House of Representatives and nine citizen members." The Smithsonian attracts nearly thirty million visitors each year. In 2018 alone, more than four million visited the NMAH.

Thus, the Greensboro counter represents a tremendous American achievement, an object, an event, and a movement of significance, both in the context of its time and in the broader context of the history of the United States. Patriotic pilgrims, by the millions, visit each year and are reminded of the importance of the counter, and the power of four young students to change the course of history.

Fath Davis Ruffins, curator of African American History and Culture at NMAH, notes that the Greensboro sit-ins were not the first or only set of sit-ins during the civil rights movement. "There were a number of sit-ins before the Greensboro sit-in. But it is fair to say that the Greensboro sit-in got a lot of attention in ways that previous sit-ins had not." In 1950, fewer than four million US households had televisions. A decade later, however, as the Greensboro sit-ins gained national attention, more than forty-five million homes,[29] nearly 90 percent of total households in the country, had a television. The movement spread rapidly.

Table 2.1. Museum Profile: National Museum of American History, Smithsonian Institution

Annual Visitors (2018)	4.1 million
Staff	257 full- and part-time employees
Budget	$40.4 million ($25M federal, $15.4M trust)
Collection	1.8 million+ objects

"National Museum of American History." Smithsonian Institution. Accessed July 17, 2019. https://www.si.edu/newsdesk/factsheets/national-museum-american-history.

The sit-ins were not just sit-ins; they represented the confluence of a number of important pieces of civic knowledge: the Civil Rights Movement, the effective organization of student protestors and activists, and the expansion of and changing impact of national televised media. The counter itself and the stories of those who made it significant, speak to a number of national themes—the power of "We the people," the march of progress and change in a democracy, the effective exercising of citizen power, and what it means to continue onward toward "a more perfect union." This moment exemplifies citizens holding America accountable to the ideals of the founding of the country. If it is a "self-evident" truth that "all men are created equal," as Jefferson claims in the Declaration, as Lincoln echoes in his "Gettysburg Address," and as Dr. Martin Luther King Jr. would later cite in his "I Have a Dream" speech, then, America, we need you to prove it to these four students, in Greensboro, NC, in February of 1960.

In the simplest of terms, four brave young men sat at a counter where they were not welcome, and in so doing, they changed the course of American history. Nearly sixty years later, this act remains important, in part because the largest, most-visited, most-funded museum of American History in the country continues to tell its story. This shows both the power and the responsibility of museums when it comes to how we share civic knowledge.

REGIONAL AND LOCAL SIGNIFICANCE

In addition to the section of the Woolworth's counter now on display at the NMAH in Washington, DC, the majority of the counter remains intact at its original site in Greensboro, North Carolina, now converted from a Woolworth's store to the International Civil Rights Center and Museum (ICRCM). A nonprofit organization named Sit-In Movement, Inc. acquired the building and worked with North Carolina Agricultural and Technical University, the college of the four protestors, to turn the space into a museum. After years of fundraising and renovation, the ICRCM opened in February 2010, marking the fiftieth anniversary of the sit-ins.

The ICRCM is a highly rated museum, averaging 4.5 out of 5 stars on Yelp as of 2019. One visitor, a Lan S. of Asheville, North Carolina, gave this

Table 2.2. Museum Profile: International Civil Rights Center and Museum

Annual Visitors	~70,000
Staff	5 full-time, 15 part-time
Budget	$862,938 (2017)
Collection	Photos, artifacts, and "the counter"

review, "I've seen a small section of the lunch counter at the Smithsonian, but seeing it here was different. For one thing, it's quite large. In its time, this must have been quite a business, and I can see why it was selected for the 1960 Greensboro sit-ins. . . . The museum is designed in a way that segregation as it existed before 1960 (and later as well), really hits home. You can see an actual 'Colored' drinking fountain, and you can see a two-sided Coca-Cola machine, where the 'white side' has cheaper drinks than the African American side—this is the 'poverty tax,' our guide explained."[30]

Whereas the counter is placed in the larger context of the national story at the NMAH, here visitors get civic knowledge that hits a little closer to home. If you lived in Greensboro, and you went to a segregated lunch counter, not only would you suffer from racial discrimination with regard to where you sat but you'd pay more for a glass of soda. Civic knowledge becomes a bit more personal. If this were a film, the exhibit at the NMAH would be the wide-establishing shot, and the counter at the ICRCM would be more of a close-up. Another reviewer on Yelp, Lisa S. of Kernersville, North Carolina, comments on the power of place, making connections between her experience as a protest marcher in 2017, and the historic significance of the location:

> The Women's March on Washington, with all its 670+ sister marches, boasting millions of people standing for something (different somethings), made a powerful statement. But of all the marches, only the Greensboro March took its thousands of marchers past the International Civil Rights Museum, the actual location of the first sit-in. The same Woolworth facade remains on the building, the same original flooring, and even the same historic lunch counter, unmoved from how it looked back in 1960.

> Dillon Tyler was our exceptional tour guide, looking into a past that is unfortunately not entirely in our past. His stories of the subliminal and overt conditioning in transportation, separate entrances, double-sided soda machines with radical markups on the Colored side . . . and I was ashamed that it took me this visit to realize for the first time that "Colored" wasn't the era's way of saying African-American, but that it was everyone not pristine white. Chinese like me. All Asians, in fact, as well as all Native Americans, and all Jews as well.

> Don't go to this museum to feel comfortable. Or to feel a sense of superiority that we've "arrived". Go to get riled up, and go do something to make the world better starting with yourself and your own home and community.[31]

For Lisa S., the experience at the museum wasn't just a look back at the history that happened fifty-seven years earlier; there was a direct connection between her experience in Greensboro in 2017 and the impact of the protestors in 1960. Informed by the lessons of history, politics, and change shared in the museum, she connects to a broader legacy of citizen changemakers in the present. She ends her review not with a wrap-up of the museum itself but with a rallying cry to others who might visit the museum. "Don't go to this museum to feel comfortable," she says. For many members of the public, civic knowledge isn't just learning facts about history and politics, it means remembering the rights and wrongs of our past. This means remembering and celebrating the achievements, the ideals, and the values of this country. But it also means being honest about where we've fallen short, and where we continue to fall short.

Dr. Will Harris, principal scholar at the International Civil Rights Center and Museum, outlined a theory of civic knowledge that is rooted in the very foundations of the country. "We have to be very careful," he said to me during a phone interview, "that civic learning and the concept of citizenship does not devolve into mere forms of action."[32] The students who led the sit-ins were animated by "constitutional principles," he pointed out. The language of the Fourteenth Amendment of the Constitution is key:

No State shall make or enforce any law which shall abridge the privileges or immunities of citizens of the United States; nor shall any State deprive any person of life, liberty, or property, without due process of law; nor deny to any person within its jurisdiction the equal protection of the laws.[33]

The students knew they had a legal right to sit at the counter. They were also motivated "by a moral sense of right and wrong," Dr. Harris noted. They were able, like any patron, to purchase food from the counter, but because the laws were not being equally applied as mandated by the Constitution, they could only take the food to go. Their protest, he notes, is not emblematic of the technique of peaceful resistance that typified the power of the civil rights movement as a whole, but a "technique of Constitutional interpretation." The students thought, "We can implement the Constitution ourselves," just by sitting down. "The true power of America," says Harris, "is always about the power of normal, everyday people."[34]

Less than half a mile away from the International Civil Rights Center and Museum, no more than a ten-minute walk past the Center City Park, is the Greensboro History Museum. Here the context is not the important chapter in national history we see at the Smithsonian, or the historic power of place we encounter at the ICRCM, but set within the context of the history of the city. Specifically, the story of the counter is in a permanent exhibit called *Voices of a City: Changing Times, 1946–1979.*

The gallery shares a series of stories about the city of Greensboro over the course of thirty-three years, three of which I'll briefly describe. Though the sit-ins represented a significant moment in both local and national history during the civil rights movement, they were not the only instance of change in

Greensboro. Here, the story of the sit-ins is one of many complicated stories of change in Greensboro. In 1948, during a polio outbreak in Greensboro, children of all races were treated together in a Greensboro polio hospital by a staff that consisted of both Black and white employees. This is long before most southern hospitals were integrated. Later, in 1963, after the Woolworth's protests had led to integrated lunch counters, students were protesting by the thousands for integration of movie theaters, hotels, and restaurants. Hundreds of these protestors were arrested and, as the local jail became overcrowded, some were incarcerated at the site of the old hospital, no longer needed because of the polio vaccines developed in the 1950s. The site now serves as a powerful reminder of both progress and regression in Greensboro. In 1979, five people who took part in an anti–Ku Klux Klan rally were shot when members of the Klan, along with Nazis, showed up and opened fire on the protestors. In two trials, no one was convicted.

At the Greensboro History Museum, the Woolworth sit-ins do not represent an ultimate triumph of justice, will, and equality; they are shown as one triumph during a tumultuous period in the history of the city that had few such moments.

THE REALM OF EXPERIENCE

When the American Alliance of Museums hosted their Annual Meeting in Atlanta in 2015, the Education Committee Professional Network, EdCom, hosted its reception at the National Center for Civil and Human Rights (NC-CHR). In addition to the speeches, networking, and appetizers, all attendees had an opportunity to explore the museum. On its website, the NCCHR bills itself as "an engaging cultural attraction that connects the American Civil Rights Movement to today's Global Human Rights Movements. The individual galleries engage visitors through a combination of powerful imagery, compelling artifacts, and poignant storytelling."[35]

A colleague who had previously been to the museum described a particular interactive in the American civil rights movement exhibit as "the most powerful museum interactive" they had ever experienced. Known simply as *Lunch Counter*, guests are first invited to learn about training for nonviolent protests before sitting at a simulation lunch counter. They "place themselves in the shoes of nonviolent protestors in 1960."

In June of 2014, Edward Rothstein wrote a review of the museum for the *New York Times* that describes the *Lunch Counter* interactive:

> The main source of the center's appeal, though, will lie in its main first floor exhibition, "Rolls Down Like Water: The American Civil Rights Movement,"

which follows the doctrines of a **museum of experience** rather than a museum of objects. It was created by the Tony Award–winning playwright and director, George C. Wolfe with exhibit design by the Rockwell Group.

The main interactive is a mock lunch counter on which you sit like the protesters of the late 1950s, wearing headphones that evoke the tumult they faced: taunts, knocks (physically felt from vibrating stools), insults—temptations to give up on nonviolent protest.[36]

Another reviewer, Jon Karmel, in a 2017 article for Picture this Post, describes the experience as follows:

We took our seats at the five-seat replica and were asked to place our hands palms down on the counter in a nonviolent pose, close our eyes and put on headphones. The later requests were to virtually simulate the experiences of the sit-in activists. For nearly two minutes we were subjected to loud and abusive threats through the headphones of recordings from the mobs that gathered at the real lunch counters more than 50 years ago. Every so often, our seats would shake, causing my heart to jump.[37]

With the previous examples of how museums explore the meaning of the Greensboro counter, we've seen it as an object of national significance set in the context of a broader national story at the Smithsonian National Museum of American History. We've seen it as a powerful example of place, faithfully restored to look as it did in 1960, telling a story of the broader civil rights movement at the International Civil Rights Center and Museum in Greensboro. And we've seen it as an object of local importance that tells part of a broader story of change in the city of Greensboro at the Greensboro History Museum. In each of these settings, however, the counter is a step removed from the visitor, behind a stanchion or barrier. The visitor is an observer to history.

At the Center in Atlanta, the approach is different. The museum wants the visitor to experience what it might have been like to sit at the lunch counter. Absent the historic objects, the visitor is invited to take a seat and have a sensory simulation of what the protestors experienced in 1960. Though the stakes are lower, there are not actual counterprotestors or members of the KKK threatening, intimidating, or physically or verbally abusing you, the museum has allowed the visitor to connect with powerful aspects of the sensory experience. When I sat in the stool and put the headphones on, I knew the experience was not real, but I still felt tension throughout my body as the insults, jeers, and kicks of the stool became increasingly violent in nature. My heart rate increased, I could feel the pounding grow with intensity in my chest, my breathing became shorter and quicker. My fight or flight response kicked in. As a frequent avoider of confrontation, I wanted nothing more than to remove the headphones and walk away. I have not before or since experienced a feeling like that in a museum. Even separated from the events by fifty-five years in an environment I knew to be safe, I was rattled for quite some time.

After the simulation ended, I got up from the stool and felt the need to talk to someone about the experience. I walked over to one of the attendants in the exhibit.

"Your simulation is so intense," I remarked. "What sorts of reactions do you generally see from your visitors?"

"Every day, I see visitors get up from the counter with tears streaming down their cheeks," she said. "Some of them are shaking. Some walk away as if they are in a daze. I think they learn in a visceral way, a way that sticks with them."

She went on to tell me the story of one of the most impactful visitor experiences she'd witnessed. "One time, a mother and son came in. They were African American. The son was maybe ten to twelve years old. They sat down at the counter together, and about thirty seconds in, the son took the headphones off and told his mom he couldn't handle it. She looked him in the eyes, and softly, but sternly, said, 'It's because those boys sat at the counter then, that you can sit here today. If they could make it through back in Greensboro, I know

Figure 2.2. Visitors to National Center for Civil and Human Rights in Atlanta sit down at the *Lunch Counter* simulation
Courtesy of the NCCHR

you can make it through a couple of minutes.' She slipped the headphones back over his ears, took his hand, and they finished the experience together."

CONCLUSION

Civic knowledge is the soil in which all aspects of citizen cultivation must be planted. For museums to fulfill their public service role, in order to help foster, connect, support, and build community, museum professionals, our visitors, and our communities must have a firm grounding in civic knowledge. Museums, better than perhaps any other source of civic knowledge, are well-equipped to share and interpret the stories, the movements, the events, the people, the places, and the information that intertwine in complex ways to form civic knowledge. We are the community gardens of democracy. Whether that knowledge is shared, gained, explored, or cocreated through objects, programs, experiences, or interactions matters slightly less.

When I was in junior high school, my social studies teacher would, when we had a substitute, assign the class to watch a BBC documentary from the late 1970s called *Connections*. At the time, my classmates and I mostly saw these days as times when we didn't have to do any real work. We were grateful, but largely disinterested. We knew it wouldn't show up on the test. Hosted by a British historian named James Burke, the gist of the series was that any single event, phenomenon, innovation, or invention did not exist in a vacuum; the history of the world is not a series of remarkable people or events but an interconnected web of people, cultures, circumstance, and innovation accelerating change.

The title of the documentary is also a great simple guide for how museums should approach the work of sharing, defining, and creating civic knowledge. Museums have both the power and the responsibility to make connections and to help the community they serve to be informed, to contemplate, and to act.

Here are three quick tips for museums and civic knowledge:

1. **Connections, Not Just Collections.** The International Civil Rights Center and Museum has one of the most powerful and iconic objects of the entire civil rights movement as part of their collection—the counter, the floors, the stools. Four young men sat down, and the world changed. However, the museum is not content to merely let the visitors see these objects. Rather, they are creating a "vision of citizenship," and a connection between this space and the constitutional legacy of our country, a connection between this space and the peaceful protests worldwide that have come in the decades since, a connection between visitors and

the ideas around what it means to be an engaged and informed citizen, and a connection between this space and the highest principles of law and morality. Civic knowledge isn't just a series of disconnected facts or a timeline of historic events. It is the soil from which citizenship should ultimately grow.

2. **The Tide Comes In, The Tide Goes Out.** At the Greensboro History Museum, the *Changing Voices* exhibit tells the story of both the success of the Greensboro sit-ins and the fierce resistance to change over time in the community. The polio hospital was integrated well before other southern hospitals during a time of crisis. The polio hospital was also used to incarcerate peaceful protestors exercising their constitutional right to peaceful assembly fifteen years later. Except in extreme circumstances, the story of a place—a home, a city, a region, or a nation—often cannot be told, in good faith, as either exclusively triumphant and celebratory, or as a shameful example of the very depths of humanity. Civic knowledge typically means wrestling with the many shades of gray that exist in between.

3. **Stories Have Morals.** There are few things less satisfying than a story without a point. The same is true for civic knowledge. For the civic knowledge to be most effective, your visitors and your community should connect the information to the present. Visitors to the International Civil Rights Center and Museum and the National Center for Civil and Human Rights make connections between the protestors in the 1960s and the instances of injustice in the world today. Ultimately, the lessons are most powerful when the visitor goes beyond comprehending the story and understands that they are part of the story. As a citizen, they have a powerful part to play, and an opportunity to star. Invite them in. Remind them that they, too, can make an impact.

NOTES

1. Center for Educational Equity, Teachers College, Columbia University. 2018. Research Summary: "Knowledge and Cognitive Skills." Edited by P. Levine. Retrieved from https://portal.civxnow.org/sites/default/files/basic_page/Research Summary-Civic Knowledge and Cognitive Skills 12-13-18.pdf.

2. National Council for the Social Studies (NCSS). 2020. "National Curriculum Standards for Social Studies: Introduction." Retrieved June 12, 2019, from https://www.socialstudies.org/standards/introduction.

3. NCSS. 2020. "National Curriculum Standards."

4. Gurian, E. H. 2007. *Civilizing the Museum: The Collected Writings of Elaine Heumann Gurian*. London: Routledge.

5. California State Board of Education. 2000. *History–Social Science Content Standards for California Public Schools: Kindergarten Through Grade Twelve*. Edited by B. Klingensmith. Sacramento: California Department of Education.

6. NCSS. 2020. "National Curriculum Standards."

7. Fingertip Facts on Education in California—CalEdFacts. August 29, 2019. Retrieved from https://www.cde.ca.gov/ds/sd/cb/ceffingertipfacts.asp.

8. Institute of Education Sciences/National Center for Education Statistics. "Digest of Education Statistics, 2013." Retrieved June 12, 2019, from https://nces.ed.gov/programs/digest/d13/tables/dt13_203.20.asp.

9. American Alliance of Museums. 2018. "Core Standards for Museums." Retrieved from https://www.aam-us.org/programs/ethics-standards-and-professional-practices/core-standards-for-museums/.

10. California State Board of Education. 2000. *History–Social Science Content Standards*.

11. National Assessment of Educational Progress (NAEP). 2018. "The Nation's Report Card: 2018 Civics." Retrieved June 10, 2019, from https://nces.ed.gov/nationsreportcard/civics/.

12. Dillon, S. 2011. "Failing Grades on Civics Exam Called a 'Crisis.'" *New York Times*, May 4, 2011. Retrieved from https://www.nytimes.com/2011/05/05/education/05civics.html

13. The Nation's Report Card. 2014. "2014 Civics Assessment: Achievement Levels: Twenty-Three Percent of Students Perform At or Above *Proficient*." Retrieved June 11, 2019, from https://www.nationsreportcard.gov/hgc_2014/#civics/achievement.

14. Davenport, D. 2019. "The Civic Education Crisis." Hoover Institution. Stanford University. Retrieved June 11, 2019, from https://www.hoover.org/research/civic-education-crisis.

15. American Council of Trustees and Alumni. 2016. *A Crisis in Civic Education*. Washington, DC. https://www.goacta.org/wp-content/uploads/ee/download/A_Crisis_in_Civic_Education.pdf.

16. Weinstein, A. 2006. "Pursuing Civic Literacy: NARA Education Programs Promote New Ways to Teach History." *Prologue* 38, no. 3 (Fall 2006). Retrieved June 12, 2019, from https://www.archives.gov/publications/prologue/2006/fall/archivist.html.

17. National Archives Foundation. 2018. "National Archives Foundation: 2018 Annual Report." Washington, DC.

18. National Center for Educational Statistics. 2013. "Digest of Education Statistics." Retrieved June 12, 2019, from https://nces.ed.gov/programs/digest/d13/tables/dt13_203.20.asp.

19. "Mission." n.d. CivXNow. Retrieved June 12, 2019, from https://www.civxnow.org/mission.

20. American Alliance of Museums (AAM). 2018. "Museum Facts & Data." Retrieved December 11, 2018, from https://www.aam-us.org/programs/about-museums/museum-facts-data/#_ednref15.

21. US Department of Education. 2018. "Department of Education: Grants to Local Educational Agencies." Washington, DC. Retrieved from https://www2.ed.gov/about/overview/budget/history/sthistbypr17.pdf.

22. AAM. 2018. "Museum Facts & Data."

23. Gurian. 2007. *Civilizing the Museum.*

24. Yeingst, William, and Lonnie Bunch. n.d. "Sitting for Justice." Originally appeared in *increase & diffusion*, Smithsonian online publication. National Museum of American History. Accessed July 1, 2019. https://amhistory.si.edu/docs/Yeingst_Bunch_Sitting_for_Justice_1996.pdf.

25. Yeingst, William. 2006. "How Did the Woolworth's Lunch Counter Become Part of NMAH's Collections?" Interview, Object of History, June 1, 2006. http://objectofhistory.org/objects/show/lunchcounter/100.

26. Gurian. 2007. *Civilizing the Museum.*

27. Gurian. 2007. *Civilizing the Museum.*

28. "National Museum of American History: Fact Sheet." n.d. Smithsonian Institution. Accessed July 17, 2019. https://www.si.edu/newsdesk/factsheets/national-museum-american-history.

29. The Buffalo History Museum. n.d. Accessed July 17, 2019. https://buffalohistory.org/explore/exhibits/virtual_exhibits/wheels_of_power/educ_materials/television.

30. S., Lan. 2018. "International Civil Rights Center & Museum—Downtown—Greensboro, NC." Yelp, January 28, 2018. Accessed July 14, 2019. https://www.yelp.com/biz/international-civil-rights-center-and-museum-greensboro.

31. S., Lisa. 2017. "International Civil Rights Center & Museum—Downtown—Greensboro, NC." Yelp, January 24, 2017. Accessed July 14, 2019. https://www.yelp.com/biz/international-civil-rights-center-and-museum-greensboro.

32. Constitution of the United States of America 1789 (rev.1992). Amendment XIV. https://www.google.com/search?q=14th+Amendment&oq=14th+Amendment&aqs=chrome..69i57.1414j0j1&sourceid=chrome&ie=UTF-8.

33. Quoted from a phone interview between Dr. Will Harris and the author.

34. Felfoldi, David. 2017. "Until . . . Telling Stories of Civil and Human Rights through Recycled Materials: Exhibit & Artists Guide." National Center for Civil and Human Rights. Accessed July 15, 2019. https://www.civilandhumanrights.org/exhibits/.

35. Quoted from a phone interview between Dr. Will Harris and the author.

36. Rothstein, Edward. 2014. "The Harmony of Liberty." *New York Times*, June 22, 2014. https://www.nytimes.com/2014/06/23/arts/design/national-center-for-civil-and-human-rights-opens-in-atlanta.html.

37. Karmel, Jon. 2017. "Atlanta Center for Civil and Human Rights Review—Stirring." Picture This Post, May 26, 2017. https://www.picturethispost.com/atlanta-center-civil-human-rights-review/.

3

Civic Mindset and The Self

I have also learnt, from experience, that the greater part of our happiness or misery depends upon our dispositions, and not upon our circumstances. We carry the seeds of the one or the other about with us, in our minds, wheresoever we go.

—Martha Washington, letter to Mercy Warren (1789)

Mindset is a bigger predictor of success than academic skills.

—Wendy Kopp, founder of Teach for America

Museums exploring their civic mission confront a set of conflicting aims. On one hand, we seek to preserve the history, the art, the knowledge, and the lessons of our collective past. On the other hand, we want to leverage these collections, the wisdom and learning of the past, to ensure the steady march of progress carries on. We stand at the precipice of the past and the future, doing our best to effectively steward both from our vantage in the present.

It can feel like we're perched upon the razor-sharp edge of a knife, torn between the simultaneous thrill and fear of hanging on and letting go, and the danger of trying to do both at once. To pull and to push; to retain the highest aims of our foundations; to embrace the changes of progress; to hold and release—this tension between conservation and progress is not exclusive to museums. It is the tension between generations. It is the tension that drives our dysfunctional politics. It is the fuel to many of our biggest fires.

The power of fuel though, lies not just in its ability to destroy and burn. Tension doesn't exist only to create anxiety. Fuel can propel us at incredible speeds toward goals we could never before reach. Tension can also provide strength and security. The challenge for museums exploring their civic mis-

43

sion is to use the fuel as propellant, and to use the tension as strength in building their communities. One of the powerful ways museums can do this is to foster civic mindset.

CIVIC MINDSET

In the first chapter of the international best-seller *The Power of Positive Thinking*, Dr. Norman Vincent Peale writes, "Believe in yourself! Have faith in your abilities! Without a humble but reasonable confidence in your own powers you cannot be successful or happy. But with sound self-confidence you can succeed. . . . Because of the importance of this mental attitude, this book will help you believe in yourself and release your inner powers."[1]

In this chapter, we'll attempt to do just that. We'll examine the ways in which museums promote, teach, cultivate, and provide space for the development of the habits of mind that contribute to engaged and informed citizenship. Or, if we're slightly bolder, and tapping into the tropes of popular culture—we'll be looking at how museums help their communities unleash their civic super powers.

"Civic and political values are a subset of the values that young people should learn, and there are no sharp lines separating the civic/political domain from others,"[2] says the Center for Educational Equity at Teachers College, Columbia University. Many of the mental habits and skills that are essential to success in school, career, and personal life, are also key to being a successful and engaged citizen. Among these are:

- Self-Awareness
- Self-Management
- Self-Efficacy/Agency
- Social Awareness
- Political Awareness
- Political Efficacy (belief that one's civic or political actions make a difference)
- Tolerance
- Empathy
- Creating/Defining Community Values

If you'll recall from chapter 1, John Cotton Dana writes that the most important thing a museum can do is to conduct "such activities as may fairly be supposed to produce beneficial effects on their respective communities." It stands to reason then, if museums conduct activities that produce beneficial effects on an individual civic mindset within a community, that those benefits extend to the broad community as well.

Let's examine some of the ways in which museums cultivate these various civic mental habits which, collectively, we'll call "civic mindset." First, I'll explore civic mindset as it pertains to an individual. Then I'll explain how civic mindset encourages an individual to better understand others. Finally, I'll discuss how these two combine to foster a broader civic mindset around a community.

THE SELF

In a March 2019 article for *Psychology Today*—"What is Self-Awareness, and How Do You Get It?"—Dr. Tchiki Davis writes, "Self-awareness involves monitoring our inner worlds, thoughts, emotions, and beliefs," and that it is "a major mechanism influencing personal development."[3] Self-awareness, which researchers say develops in humans at roughly eighteen months of age, corresponds to the acquisition and use of verbal communication. As we become aware of ourselves, we want others to know about it. In the earliest stages, self-awareness allows us to shift from being dependent to independent. We become our own person with our own wants and needs and emotions. And we aren't afraid to let those around us know it.

Self-awareness is also a trait that predicts success later in life. A 2019 study by Cornell University's School of Industrial and Labor Relations and Green Peak Partners, called "What Predicts Executive Success?", showed that the stereotypical, type A, uncompromising executives and leaders who relentlessly focus on results actually perform worse that leaders who are self-aware. "Our findings," said J. P. Flaum of Green Peak Partners, "directly challenge the conventional view that 'drive for results at all costs' is the right approach. The executives most likely to deliver good bottom line results are actually self-aware leaders who are especially good at working with individuals and in teams."[4] In fact, the study showed that the single biggest predictor of leadership success was a high self-awareness score.

The better you understand yourself, the better you are able to build on your strengths and work with others to minimize your weaknesses. This is the second shift in self-awareness. Just as a toddler must shift from a dependent person to an independent person, in order for independent citizens to become contributing members of a broader community, they must mentally shift from a mindset of independence to interdependence. This holds true regardless of how you define your community—personal, familial, professional, regional, national, etc.

Leadership success stemming from self-awareness is not exclusive to the corporate world. In fact, it is one of the key traits that made Abraham Lincoln such a success. Lincoln, who, according to a 2017 C-SPAN poll[5] of more than ninety eminent historians rated as the greatest presidential leader in the history of the United States, faced quite a challenge. Historian Doris Kearns Goodwin, in her book *Leadership in Turbulent Times*, described the situation as follows:

> When Abraham Lincoln entered the presidency on March 4, 1861, the house was not merely divided; the house was on fire. In the four months between his election and inauguration, seven southern states had passed resolutions to secede from the union. . . . From the start, Lincoln correctly identified the full gravity of the challenge the secession posed to the continued existence of his country's communal life, its shared experiences, its memories, its role as a beacon of hope to the world at large.[6]

As he assumed the highest elected leadership role in the country, his national community faced the most significant national threat it had yet endured. A leader who was less self-aware might think they could solve this on their own. They might delegate quickly and demand results, placing themselves at the center of the storm alone. Not Lincoln.

> Lincoln created a team of independent, strong-minded men, all of whom were more experienced in public life, better educated, and more celebrated than he. In the top three positions, at the State Department, the Treasury, and the Justice Department, he placed his three chief rivals—William Seward, Salmon Chase, and Edward Bates—each of whom thought he should be president instead of the prairie lawyer from Illinois.[7]

Lincoln was profoundly self-aware. He knew the enormity of the problem he faced could not be borne alone.

In Stephen R. Covey's seminal work, *The 7 Habits of Highly Effective People,* he points out that the shift from dependence to independence is a *private victory*, and the shift from independence to interdependence is a *public victory*. Lincoln leveraged the talents and abilities of his cabinet and beyond to assure the largest public victory in the history of the United States—the preservation of the union. Just as this shift to interdependence was crucial for the survival of our national community, it is essential to a field concerned with creating a public benefit. So for museums to support students, visitors, and their communities in becoming more self-aware means that they are contributing to a public victory. They are crafting their public benefit.

So how do museums do this? How can they do it better?

The Student Leadership Program is a week-long summer program for high school students that takes place on-site at the Ronald Reagan Presidential

Library. The program focuses on three core tenets that we believe will support students as they strive to become the civic-minded leaders of the future: effective communication, civic duty, and informed decision-making. Over the course of the week, students identify an issue in their community that they would like to help solve, put together a detailed leadership action plan, and on the final day they pitch their plan to an adult community leader they have not met. As a result of this program, students have started antibullying clubs, put together financial literacy seminars, started their own 501(c)(3) charities, and completed well over one hundred different service projects. They have worked with their fellow students, teachers, administrators, public officials, and community leaders to craft public victories.

A big component of the program is building self-awareness. Early in the program, students are asked to assess themselves using a Personality Compass.[8] The compass is used as a self-assessment tool and is particularly apt for helping students both to better understand their own style of leadership as well as open their eyes to other styles of leadership. It is one of many self-assessments you might implement including Myers-Briggs, or a DISC (dominance, influence, steadiness, conscientiousness) assessment. The general gist is that by answering a set of questions, you learn a little bit more about the type of person you are, and in turn you learn how to self-manage the aspects of your personality style so that you can work effectively with folks who have other styles.

The compass assessment is also used by the Corporation for National and Community Service, which includes Americorps, whose mission is "committed to improving lives, strengthening communities, and fostering civic engagement through service and volunteering." So for those looking to build self-awareness in service-minded leaders, using a tool that the Americorps uses to support eighty thousand volunteers annually seems like a good place to start. The basic premise is that people have a variety of different personality styles that impact how they lead and work with others. These include:

- **North: The General.** These are assertive, decisive, confident leaders. They are results oriented, believe in the power of their ideas, and have no problem assuming control of the situation. You often find these types of personalities in leadership positions, though you'll recall the research from Green Peak Partners suggests this type of leader doesn't always get the best results.
- **South: The Nurturer.** These leaders are likable team-oriented leaders. We might identify them as servant leaders because they are generous, not too competitive, and take joy from the success of others on their team. They are more concerned with equity and fairness than just getting

something done. You might find a few of this type of personality in the education field.

- **East: The Visionary.** These leaders are focused on big ideas and concepts, enjoy the process of being creative, and are driven by mission and purpose. Often these types of leaders are incredibly spiritual and believe in limitless possibility. They might also be a bit more spontaneous and adventurous and open to new experiences and risks.
- **West: The Analyst.** The Western personality is more concerned with data, rules, regulations, and logic. This type of leader might be exceptional at developing and following procedures. They are deliberative and use data to drive decision-making.

After answering a series of questions, students find themselves at a certain set of grid coordinates. It could be one of the four main compass directions, but many people are a mixture of styles—such as a northeast visionary general or a nurturing analyst from the southwest quadrant. The way you lead, the types of professions or activities that might appeal to you—these can all be connected to personality types.

I chatted with Ruben Lugo, coordinator for the Student Leadership Program. Full disclosure, Ruben is a colleague of mine, and one that I admire. He is a fantastic museum educator. Soft-spoken and thoughtful, Ruben has an ease about him, and cares deeply about ensuring that each and every student feels welcome when they come on campus, regardless of ability, background, ethnicity, socioeconomic status, or anything else. As an educator working with students during the program, and as the person charged with coordinating the program as a whole, he has seen its impact on students.

"We like to have them do a self-assessment before they take the Personality Compass," he says. "So we'll hand out the compass, explain the different styles of personality, and have them predict where they will end up. A lot of the students are pretty self-aware. They end up being pretty close, but many of them are way off. Their perception doesn't always match the reality."

In addition to very specific programmatic assessments that help visitors develop self-awareness, there are many other ways in which museums can and do promote a better understanding of the self.

Dr. Tchiki Davis offers a number of suggestions for how people can help build their own self-awareness, two of which museums are well-positioned to build into their programs or encourage:

1. **"Walking, especially in the quiet of nature, can be useful in building self-awareness."** It is easy for the modern person to spend very little time thinking about the self. In fact, according to a 2016 report

by the Nielson Company, the average American spends more than ten hours a day looking at a screen. With the explosive growth of devices: computers, televisions, smartphones, tablets, watches, video games, etc. fewer and fewer Americans take time to unplug, connect with nature, and reflect. A number of botanic gardens across the country offer the chance to commune with nature, or to unplug and meditate on your own or with a group. If your museum has a garden, courtyard, or outdoor space, you might consider offering visitors the chance to quietly connect with the world around them. In creating quiet spaces, not only can visitors connect with nature, they can spend some time connecting with themselves.

2. **"Self-awareness can open your mind to new perspectives."** Dr. Davis writes, "We each tend to have different perspectives on a variety of topics, but as we develop these perspectives, we get comfortable with them and have a preference for our own opinions. However, limited perspectives lead to limited thinking, so by being open to the views of others, we can expand our perspectives to be more universally inclusive. New ideas are refreshing and stimulating, opening our thinking in new and possibly promising directions."[9] In addition to providing a space for contemplation that could lead to better self-awareness, or providing programming or interactive elements that directly promote self-awareness, museums also need to recognize that each visitor comes into a museum experience deeply entrenched in their own narrative. Museums, as "institutions of memory" often offer their own narrative, or present a clash of perspectives and narratives.

We must realize that each interaction between a visitor and museum is a clash of narratives. As John Falk writes in "Understanding Museum Visitors' Motivations and Learning":

> Time and time again, what leaps out . . . is how deeply personal museum visits are, and how deeply tied to each individual's sense of identity. Also striking is how consistently an individual's post-visit narrative relates to their entering narrative. In other words, what typically sticks in a person's mind as important about their visit usually directly relates to the reasons that person stated they went to the museum in the first place. . . . The ways in which individuals talk about why they went to the museum as well as the ways they talk about what they remember from their experience invariably seem to have a lot to do with what they were seeking to personally accomplish through their visit. Visitors talk about how their personal goals for the visit relate to who they thought they were or wanted to be, and they talk about how the museum itself supported these personal goals and needs.[10]

To help contribute to the crafting of thoughtful, engaged, self-aware citizens, museums must strive to be weavers of narrative. In a sense, we are the confluence of our subject matter narrative, the narrative with which the visitor enters and exits the museum, and the broader narrative of the community, and history. To some degree, in order to effectively fulfill our civic mission, we have to think of our work like a showrunner for an epic miniseries. How will we tie the strands of these different pieces together? How will we connect the main story and the subplots, the diverse characters with radically different sets of motivations? Museums are very concerned with the idea of connecting the self-aware visitor to "new perspectives."

In fact, a Google search of "new perspectives" and "museum exhibit" returns more than 1.8 million results. This includes New Perspectives Tours at the New Museum of New York, an exhibit called *N. C. Wyeth: New Perspectives* at the Brandywine River Museum of Art, a New Perspectives Case at the National Museum of American History that highlights new objects and stories in the collection, and an exhibit *Outside Eyes: New Perspectives on the Collection* at the Taubman Museum of Art in Virginia. Let me be clear. Museums excel at presenting new perspectives through art, historical narrative, the impact of the sciences and more. It is the ability to connect these new perspectives, to weave them into the narrative of the visitor, that is ultimately one of the key factors determining how successful a museum is in fulfilling its civic mission. There must be a "stickiness factor."

Not only are museums individually concerning themselves with ways to connect with the self-narrative of our visitors, but museums, as a field, are increasingly focusing on the importance of self-awareness as well. In the 2018 report, *Facing Change*, the American Alliance of Museums expounded on why they made DEAI (Diversity, Equity, Access, and Inclusion) the first focus area of their organizational strategic plan for 2016–2020. "Diversity, equity, accessibility, and inclusion are essential, sustainable values for museums to pursue. These principles are not only bedrocks of ethical and morally courageous museum work, but they also signal how the field can remain relevant to an ever-diversifying US population,"[11] write the authors of the study. Both the process for putting this report together and the first of the five key insights are directly connected to better understanding the self.

The very first recommendation of the working group is that "every museum professional must do personal work to face unconscious bias." Just as developing a civic mindset begins with first understanding the self, so, too, does the task of the museum field at large when faced with the task of maintaining relevancy in an increasingly diverse and divided country. We must, as a field and as individual practitioners, become more self-aware of our own strengths, weaknesses, thoughts, biases, and preconceived notions.

Here's the challenge for the museum field: we must simultaneously do this work on our own (and I encourage you to read the report and implement the recommendations for trainings, assessments, and conversations within your department and institution) while fostering an environment where our visitors and community can actively become more self-aware as well.

Second, they described the process the group went through in researching and issuing the report. "In the working group meetings, *we committed to a process of self-reflection*, learning from past efforts, recognizing the barriers that have hindered the field's progress, and breaking down those barriers in specific ways. We also agreed that no person or organization can do this work alone. Every museum service organization, museum, and individual has work to do. If we make progress, it is because we have all played a part." This shift is key. In order for any community to successfully respond to the challenges it faces, whether a working group hosted by AAM, a meditation group at a botanical garden, students collaborating to end bullying at their school, or an elected official and his cabinet trying to stem the dissolution of his country, there must be the ability to connect the self to others. There must be a shift from independence to interdependence. In the next chapter, we'll explore how museums shift from mindset to developing the civic skills necessary to make an impact.

NOTES

1. Peale, Norman Vincent. 2008. *The Power of Positive Thinking*. New York: Fireside/Simon & Schuster.

2. Center for Educational Equity, Teachers College, Columbia University. 2018. Research Summary: "Values, Dispositions and Attitudes, December 2018." Retrieved from https://portal.civxnow.org/sites/default/files/resources/Research%20Summary -Values%20Dispositions%20and%20Attitudes%2012-13-18.pdf.

3. Davis, Tchiki. 2019. "What Is Self-Awareness, and How Do You Get It?" *Psychology Today*, March 11, 2019. https://www.psychologytoday.com/us/blog/click -here-happiness/201903/what-is-self-awareness-and-how-do-you-get-it.

4. American Management Association. 2019. "New Study Shows Nice Guys Finish First." AMA, January 24, 2019. https://www.amanet.org/articles/new-study -shows-nice-guys-finish-first/.

5. C-SPAN. "Total Scores/Overall Rankings: C-SPAN Presidential Historians Survey, 2017." Accessed August 15, 2019. https://www.c-span.org/presidentsurvey 2017/?page=overall.

6. Goodwin, Doris Kearns. 2018. *Leadership in Turbulent Times*. New York: Simon & Schuster.

7. Goodwin. 2018. *Leadership in Turbulent Times*.

8. "Leadership Compass." Corporation for National and Community Service. Accessed August 19, 2019. https://www.nationalservice.gov/sites/default/files/resource/leadershipcompass.pdf.

9. Davis. 2019. "What is Self-Awareness?"

10. Falk, John. "Understanding Museum Visitors' Motivations and Learning." *Motivation and Learning Styles*, 106–27. Accessed August 19, 2019. https://slks.dk/fileadmin/user_upload/dokumenter/KS/institutioner/museer/Indsatsomraader/Brugerundersoegelse/Artikler/John_Falk_Understanding_museum_visitors__motivations_and_learning.pdf.

11. American Alliance of Museums. 2018. "Facing Change: Insights from the American Alliance of Museums' Diversity, Equity, Accessibility, and Inclusion Working Group." Arlington, VA: American Alliance of Museums. https://www.aam-us.org/wp-content/uploads/2018/04/AAM-DEAI-Working-Group-Full-Report-2018.pdf.

A Tale of Three Cities: Civic Skills

It takes collaboration across a community to develop better skills for better lives.

—José Ángel Gurría

Talent you have naturally. Skill is only developed by hours and hours of work.

—Usain Bolt

In previous chapters, we've explored how museums play a vital civic role in preserving and sharing civic knowledge and developing vital components of the mental habits of effectively engaged citizens. In this chapter, we'll further explore how museums work to instill essential civic skills. We'll visit Durham, New Hampshire, to see how the Museum of Art at the University of New Hampshire is working to build skills in civil discourse. We'll then go across the country, to the streets of San Francisco, to see the ways in which the iconic Exploratorium works with city and community partners to use science to build civic collaboration skills through their Studio for Public Spaces. Then we'll do a deep dive into the Great Communicator Debate Series, a national program put on by the Annenberg Presidential Learning Center at the Ronald Reagan Presidential Foundation and Institute that partners with the National Speech and Debate Association and high schools from across the country to help develop research and communication skills.

DURHAM, NEW HAMPSHIRE: AN ART MUSEUM
IN THE EYE OF THE POLITICAL STORM

New Hampshire has a long, proud history of civic engagement. In 1776, it was the first of the American colonies to establish an independent government, and the first to ratify a colonial constitution. In 1784, three years prior to the creation of the United States Constitution, New Hampshire updated their constitution and introduced a Bill of Rights. Their state motto, "Live Free or Die," is emblazoned on the license plate of every vehicle in the state, and is embodied in Article 7 of the New Hampshire Bill of Rights:

> The people of this State have the sole and exclusive right of governing themselves as a free, sovereign, and independent State; and do, and forever hereafter shall, exercise and enjoy every power, jurisdiction, and right, pertaining thereto, which is not, or may not hereafter be, by them expressly delegated to the United States of America in Congress assembled.[1]

So concerned are the residents of New Hampshire with effective governance that they are one of the few states in the country to have included a Right of Rebellion in their state constitution. Article 10 states, "Whenever the ends of government are perverted, and public liberty manifestly endangered, and all other means of redress are ineffectual, the people may, and of right ought to reform the old, or establish a new government."

To say that residents of New Hampshire take their freedom and their role as citizens seriously is an understatement.

New Hampshire is also small.

In terms of size, New Hampshire ranks forty-fifth of the fifty states, between Vermont and New Jersey, with 9,351 total square miles. As a point of comparison, Alaska, the largest state, measures more than 650,000 square miles. With a population of roughly 1.3 million, it ranks forty-first. Since 1884, it has been consistent in terms of its electoral impact, with an allocation of four electoral votes. This ranks forty-third. Seven states and the District of Columbia have three electoral votes. Combining New Hampshire with the twenty-four electoral votes from the states and DC would equal twenty-eight, roughly half the electoral power that California wields. Since 1912, New Hampshire has been nearly evenly split on how it votes presidentially, having fifteen times voted for a Republican, and twelve times going to the Democratic candidate. Since 1964, the state split has been an even 7–7. Despite the relative toss-up nature of the state, presidential candidates spend a lot more time in states like Florida (twenty-nine electoral votes), Pennsylvania (twenty), and Ohio (eighteen) during the run-up to the general election.

Yet this tiny state with a long history of independence and civic engagement arguably wields more power in determining the president of the United

States than any other state. It's because, much like their constitution, they like to get an early start on their civic engagement.

By tradition, since 1920,[2] and by law since the 1970s, New Hampshire has the first set of primary elections in the country. At various points in electoral history, other states and the political parties have attempted to shift bigger states with more delegates to earlier in the election cycle, but New Hampshire authorized its secretary of state to move elections to preserve its first-in-the-nation status. Now, other states are penalized for trying to move ahead of New Hampshire, and the electoral timeline of Iowa caucuses followed by New Hampshire primaries has become tradition. As a result, the national and international media descend upon New Hampshire with each primary season.

So it is no surprise that this small, independent, and civically engaged state wields a tremendous amount of civic power.

In fact, according to one study, a win in the New Hampshire primary will increase a candidate's share of primary votes in all other states by as much as 27 percent.[3] With millions of potential voters watching in other states across the country, New Hampshire is, to borrow a term from social media, an influencer. On the Democratic side, New Hampshire voters have voted in favor of four of the last six Democratic candidates, with Senator Obama coming in a close second to Hillary Clinton in 2008, and Bernie Sanders defeating Clinton in 2016. On the Republican side, New Hampshire voters have selected the ultimate party nominee in four of the last five elections.

Figure 4.1.   The Balsams Grand Resort Hotel in Dixville, New Hampshire—site of some of the earliest polling results in the country
Photo by P199

Perhaps no place in New Hampshire exemplifies this spirit of small, influential, and first better than tiny Dixville Notch. Located roughly twenty miles south of the Canadian border, Dixville Notch recorded a population of just twelve residents during the 2010 census. During both the primary and general elections, Dixville Notch holds its elections at midnight. The registered voters in the town gather in the Ballot Room at The Balsams Grand Resort Hotel, formerly a vast ski resort that could house up to four hundred guests, but since 2011, it has been shuttered except for those who wish to cast their votes. In 2016, CNN and Fox News broadcast live coverage of the voting in Dixville Notch, and dozens of news outlets from around the world shared the results with millions of people. The final tally of the nine residents who cast their votes: on the Democratic side, Senator Bernie Sanders received all four votes. On the Republican side, Senator John Kasich received three, and Donald Trump two.

All this attention doesn't come without scandal. One of the viewers recognized his neighbor, a man who did not live in Dixville Notch, being interviewed and reported it to the state attorney general. The resulting investigation revealed that some of the midnight voters didn't actually live in Dixville Notch, some having moved away in the 1980s. As a result, the Dixville Notch voter checklist is down to five people, and Dixville Notch might not have enough people to staff their polling place in 2020. I told you New Hampshirites take their civic duty seriously.[4]

Just over three hours away from Dixville Notch is the University of New Hampshire. Kristina Durocher is the director of the Museum of Art at UNH.

"New Hampshire is a place that has always prided itself on its civic engagement," says Durocher. Because of its importance in the presidential primary cycle, citizens have the opportunity to interact with potential future presidents of the United States in the living room of local house parties. "It is," she says, "an unusual situation for your average citizen to find themselves in."

In fact, the auditorium at her institution is often used by candidates from both parties. In February 2016, the University of New Hampshire cosponsored the Democratic primary debate. It was the first one-on-one between Hillary Clinton and Bernie Sanders. Durocher's office served as the hold room for debate moderator Rachel Maddow of MSNBC—truly a front row seat to the democratic process.

At the macro level, New Hampshire is a powerful example of what civic engagement can look like. But I want to be clear, civic engagement is not and should not be defined only by what happens at the highest levels of civic participation. As much attention as presidential elections and presidential candidates receive, what happens at the ground level of civic engagement is just as, if not more, important. After all, not every museum is in an early primary state. Not every museum employee's office will be used to house moderators or candidates for the highest office in the land.

In order to be engaged and informed participants in democracy, citizens should do more than just cast a vote every four years. Casting a vote isn't a skill, it's an act. It's an important act, absolutely, and one that, in the aggregate, has a powerful impact on how our national, state, and local governments operate. Of all the ways to be civically engaged, it is also, arguably, the easiest. The voters who gather in Dixville Notch to cast the first votes in the primary and general elections are typically done in just a few short minutes. Though it is better to be informed on a candidate or an issue when casting a vote, there is no requirement for a voter to have done any research, to gather any knowledge, or to survey various positions before voting. One could vote completely at random, like a high school student taking a standardized test, and there would be no consequences for the voter.

When it is time to vote, social media is flooded with images of voters who proudly display their "I Voted" sticker, and who rack up likes and heart emojis for their display of civic engagement. Even though it is the easiest and most common form of civic participation, it doesn't mean we do it well. In 2016, 55.7 percent of the voting-age population turned out to vote in the presidential election. According to Pew Research,[5] the United States ranks twenty-six of thirty-two "highly developed, democratic states" in terms of voter turnout. In other words, nearly half of our voting-age population is either unable, disenfranchised, too busy, too lazy, too uninformed, or too bored to participate in the *easiest* form of civic engagement. Besides, just voting isn't nearly enough.

"Self-government requires far more than voting in elections every four years. It requires citizens who are informed and thoughtful, participate in their communities, are involved in the political process, and possess moral and civic virtues. Generations of leaders, from America's founders to the inventors of public education to elected leaders in the twentieth century, have understood that these qualities are not automatically transmitted to the next generation—they must be passed down"[6] says the 2011 *Guardian of Democracy* report.

So how can museums build the civic skills that lead to increased engagement in their communities? How can museums help develop skills that also teach moral and civic virtues? New Hampshire, a state whose turnout rate of roughly 70 percent[7] is one of the top three in the country offers a way.

"New Hampshire is small, only 1.3 million people or so, so it's more like a giant town or city," says Kristina Durocher. With the largest legislative body of any state in the country, and the fourth largest in the English-speaking world[8] (trailing only the British Parliament, the US Congress, and the Canadian Parliament), most New Hampshirites "know their representatives and have a street level view of civic engagement. In fact, citizens can often go through town budgets on a line by line basis."[9]

While the citizens of New Hampshire are good at citizen budgetary analysis, they needed some work in the area of civil discourse. This is not unique to either New Hampshire, the University of New Hampshire, or the Museum of Art. In fact, Americans are increasingly frustrated and experience increased levels of stress when discussing political issues with those with different viewpoints. A 2017 study by the American Psychological Association reports that "nearly six in 10 adults (59 percent) report that the current social divisiveness causes them stress when thinking about the nation."[10] And according to Pew Research, "53% of Americans say talking about politics with people they disagree with is generally stressful and frustrating."[11] So in this environment of deteriorating and increasingly stressful discourse, the way the Museum of Art is leveraging its resources and partnering across the university and the community provides a great example of how other museums might collaborate to address the important skill of civil discourse.

In May 2017, a controversy erupted on the campus of the University of New Hampshire following Cinco de Mayo. Several students "celebrated" the holiday by donning sombreros, fake moustaches, and drinking heavily. In response, a group formed and said, "Students who celebrate with sombreros, fake mustaches and ponchos are appropriating Mexican culture."[12] The university then convened a forum to discuss the controversy and racial tension on campus. According to *The New Hampshire*, UNH's independent student newspaper, "Many students left feeling unsatisfied with the discussion, and felt like their voices were unheard."[13]

As a result, the university convened a task force, and realized the campus needed a way for people to convene and discuss tough issues. They needed to improve discourse. Around the same time, the Department of Communication launched its Civil Discourse Lab (CDL)—an extension of the curriculum they teach in their courses on dialogue, deliberation, and collaboration. The CDL's mission is to strengthen "the ability of our students and community members to conduct meaningful conversations, collaborate, and weigh decisions around sometimes difficult but important topics to a civil society through research, engaged teaching and praxis."[14]

Durocher explains that the museum saw an opportunity to partner with the CDL in conjunction with an upcoming exhibit of the photography of Yoav Horesh called *Aftermath*. The photographer, an Israeli, lived in the United States during 9/11 and was "struck by how different the American response, with its grounded planes and makeshift memorials, was from his own experiences in Israel. While the American impulse was to 'never forget,' Israel's urge was to erase."[15] The exhibit consisted of sites from more than twenty-five suicide bombings and was concerned with "trauma, violence, and collective memory."

Durocher knew that the exhibit "could make some people upset." And, if there is one thing we aren't terribly good at as a society in the age of Twitter, it is having productive discussions about tough topics. Durocher felt that art provided an opportunity to build this necessary civic skill. The CDL trains students to facilitate discussions. Students both attended lectures on campus promoting the power of dialogue and also worked with professors and CDL directors Renee Heath and Jennifer Borda and guests to have powerful public conversations. One such guest was Sallyann Roth from the dialogue-convening organization, Essential Partners. Roth shared her storied experience bringing together people from "opposite sides of the abortion debates as a way of building empathy and acknowledging the complexity of the topic."[16] Students learn techniques for building programs and facilitating difficult conversations.

Durocher felt that art and photography offer a powerful grounding in complex topics. In an age of dialogue where much of the discourse we see modeled by politicians and the Twitterverse is reactionary, absolute, immediate, and zero sum, Durocher wanted to leverage the exhibition to teach students and the community to think deeply, to learn how to have a complex discussion about a complex topic, and to simply be better at having a tough conversation.

So the museum worked with the CDL to host two programs and a facilitated discussion after the screening of a film in conjunction with the exhibit. Durocher admitted that this first foray into civil discourse did not turn out as expected. "The first set of talks were not as well attended as we hoped," she said, but "we are still building the program and developing a deeper partnership with the CDL." The dialogues are structured in a very specific way to focus on building empathy. Discussion participants are actively invited to disagree, but are reminded to be respectful and share each other's stories. In this way, the discussion is not only focused on the topics or the ideas but also on respecting the people who hold the ideas and their lived experience that contributes to the thinking behind the ideas. In short, these discussions build empathy and give context. The discussions also leverage the exhibit to make broader connections to the world beyond the exhibit.

In an increasingly polarized world, what does peace look like to you?

What does a democratic, just, open, multiethnic, and sustainable society look like?

Thus, the civil discourse promoted in the discussion invites students to start with themselves, ground themselves in personal experience and reaction, and then connect beyond their personal experience to a shared experience.

Figure 4.2. Norman Rockwell's *Freedom of Speech*
U.S. National Archives and Records Administration

This is how civil discourse happens—with respect and empathy for those whose lived experience is different.

After her first experience with the CDL, Durocher partnered with For Freedoms, a national, nonpartisan organization that "believes citizenship is defined by participation, not by ideology." For Freedoms uses "art as a vehicle for participation to deepen public discussions on civic issues and core values."[17] The organization makes a direct connection between Franklin Roosevelt's "Four Freedoms" speech and art. In the speech, Roosevelt describes a world founded on four basic human freedoms—freedom of speech, freedom of worship, freedom from want, and freedom from fear. Inspired by the speech, artist Norman Rockwell created a series of paintings in 1943 that appeared in the *Saturday Evening Post* and helped generate millions of sales of war bonds during World War II.

Figure 4.3. Norman Rockwell's *Freedom of Worship*
U.S. National Archives and Records Administration

Figure 4.4. Norman Rockwell's *Freedom from Want*
U.S. National Archives and Records Administration

Durocher was drawn to the organization because it fosters civil discourse and engagement in democracy through interactions with art and artists. For Freedoms proudly claims to have "launched the largest creative collaboration in our nation's history, the 50 State Initiative." In the 2018 midterms they "held over 600 concurrent decentralized public events across the country with over 250 partners that reflected a multiplicity of voices and sparked a national dialogue about art, education, commerce, and politics."[18] One of these activations was at the Museum of Art at UNH.

Students and representatives of clubs and organizations were invited to create yard signs. Whereas the yard signs looked like traditional political yard signs we see in the lead-up to local and state elections, instead of advocating for a particular politician or ballot measure, students were invited to complete one of four prompts: "Freedom to," "Freedom from," "Freedom for," or "Freedom of." After the students created their signs, they were installed around campus for one month.

In its initial year, the signs were installed mainly in the natural, woodsy, area on campus that surrounded the museum. Students created more than

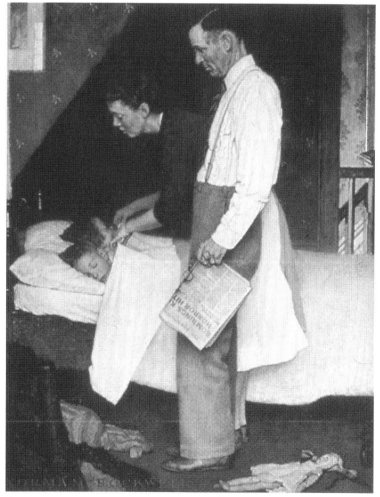

Figure 4.5. Norman Rockwell's *Freedom from Fear*
U.S. National Archives and Records Administration

Figure 4.6.   Student designed "Freedom" signs at UNH
Photo courtesy of Kristina Durocher, UNH

a hundred signs, and the CDL analyzed common themes that appeared. These themes then served as the basis of a public forum, a town hall–type meeting designed and facilitated by the students from the CDL. Special invitations were extended to student political organizations, who sought a space to engage together across their perceived differences. To foster such dialogue, the forum design shifted them away from debating positions and, instead, engaged them around shared values and personal experiences. During the dialogue, participants reflected on notions of freedom derived from the yard signs, shared how their understanding of freedom informed their political beliefs, and deliberated about how freedoms are both fostered and challenged by our contemporary, contentious political climate.

"Having something concrete is important when discussing abstract ideas," says Durocher. "Having photographs, or yard signs, or art gives people a baseline for a difficult discussion."

I asked Durocher about how one could assess the impact of these programs, activities, and discussions.

"How do you measure success?"

"The program is still in its relative infancy," she says. "There aren't yet any specific metrics or data points or in-depth studies on the impact of these civil discussions. But the yard signs really do a great job of getting people talking."

In a polarized age where folks do a much better job of talking over and around each other, a good conversation inspired by art might, in and of itself, be just the outcome we're looking for.

SAN FRANCISCO, CALIFORNIA: USING SCIENCE TO BRING PEOPLE TOGETHER

On the other side of the country, at the edge of the cool Pacific waters, sits one of America's iconic cities. Founded originally in the civically important year of 1776, it became the largest town on the West Coast by the end of the 1849 gold rush. San Francisco has a long reputation as a thriving center of civic engagement. In the 1960s, its Haight-Ashbury district was often credited with being the birthplace of the hippie movement. During 1967's "Summer of Love" more than one hundred thousand people moved to San Francisco as the social order shifted drastically across America, and "free love, drug use and communal living became the norm."[19]

In terms of civic engagement, San Francisco has long been a center of liberal activism. As a city, it last voted for a Republican presidential candidate in 1956 with Dwight D. Eisenhower.[20] In 2016, Hillary Clinton received nearly 85 percent of the vote in San Francisco. It is the city that elected Harvey Milk, the first openly gay official in the history of California, in the late seventies. And Gavin Newsom, California's current governor, made international news in 2004 when he began granting same-sex wedding licenses, a full eleven years before the US Supreme Court ruled that same-sex marriages were legal in all fifty states. In addition to its reputation as being a national leader for civic engagement and civic change, the City by the Bay is home to many of Silicon Valley's most recognizable companies, the Golden Gate Bridge, and many world-class museums and attractions. In short, it is a city rich in history, culture, and civic passion, vibrant with commerce and tourism. It is a city alive.

That said, like any densely populated major city, it is not without civic issues. One of the most polarizing is the city's struggle with homelessness. An October 2019 article in the *San Francisco Chronicle* sums up the issue, "On Monday, there were 1,078 people on the waiting list for shelter in San Francisco, a city with a $12.3 billion annual budget and the highest density of billionaires of any city in the world. No. 22 on the list for a cot is 77 years old."[21]

Residents of the Clinton Park neighborhood, fed up with tent encampments, drug use, and violence in front of their homes, purchased twenty-four large boulders to line their sidewalk to encourage the homeless population to move elsewhere. What ensued was a tragicomic symphony of civic engagement. At night, homeless activists would gather and shove the boulders into the streets. During the day, residents would call the Department of Public Works to move the boulders back in place. Each night the cycle would repeat itself. It was the myth of Sisyphus come to life. And no one was happy. Heather Knight, the author of the article, spoke to one of the residents.

> "Those of us who are living here have a right to not have people pooping in front of our door," she said. "And the people living in the streets have a right to live like humans and not have to defecate on the sidewalks."

Like many political issues in the modern world, the issue became intense and binary. If you were for the homeless, you must be against the wealthy and selfish homeowners. If you were for the peaceful property owners looking to feel safe in front of their homes, you must be against the violent, drug-using homeless population. But many can't understand why it has to be binary. Knight continues, "They don't understand why not wanting a drug den outside your home makes you anti-homeless. And they don't understand why super-rich San Francisco can't provide more shelter beds, supportive housing units, drug treatment, mental health care and mandated treatment for those too ill to know they need it."[22]

Sometimes the issue isn't lighting a civic fire where none exists, and encouraging the disengaged to participate. Sometimes the issue is about cohesion. How can museums leverage their civic power to help bring people together for the common good? In San Francisco, there is not a civic engagement problem. However, for some issues, there is a problem when it comes to bringing people together to work on complicated solutions. This is not unique to San Francisco by any stretch. But if you can't bring people together in a city where 85 percent of the population is politically aligned, how can we, in an era of hyperpartisanship, "cancel culture," and intense online reactions to nearly everything, find ways to work together?

Perhaps museums offer an answer. Elaine Heumann Gurian writes, "I steadfastly believe that museums can foster societal cohesion and civility. Taking museums' community-building role seriously is not easy and requires multifaceted and consistent commitment."[23] In San Francisco, there is a museum, with a decades-long reputation for approaching teaching in innovative ways, that might just have a solution on how to leverage museums to bring people together.

Sitting at the edge of San Francisco, on Pier 15, roughly a mile from the stretch of Interstate 80 (curiously enough called the Dwight D. Eisenhower

Highway) that becomes the Bay Bridge and links San Francisco to Oakland, is the iconic Exploratorium. Founded by physicist Frank Oppenheimer, whose previous work included the Manhattan Project,[24] the Exploratorium is renowned for its hands-on, interactive, inquiry-based approach to learning. Edward Rothstein of the *New York Times* wrote that the Exploratorium is "the most important science museum to have opened since the mid-twentieth century because of the nature of its exhibits, its wide-ranging influence and its sophisticated teacher training program."[25]

Rothstein goes on to explain the principles of exploration that drove Oppenheimer to create the Exploratorium, "Here, sufficiently well-understood science has nothing magical about it. Science is comprehended not through abstract principles but through concrete experience. It is revealed not through speculation but through manipulation. You learn by exploring."

So, what if you take these same principles and apply them to the art of civic engagement? Rather than a didactic exhibit that explains the importance of being civically engaged, or label copy that describes why communication is important in politics, or an illuminating video on the power of people coming together to solve a problem, what if a museum created a space for people to explore these concepts through experience?

I spoke with Shawn Lani, the director of the Studio for Public Spaces at the Exploratorium. Shawn is an artist and curator who has been charged with "developing and installing public works throughout the Bay Area." He is passionate that the work of the museum must extend beyond its mere walls, "Museums can't just measure their impact by how many people come through the doors. A museum should not just be a building. A museum is an institution that should have a positive impact on the lives of others, no matter where that might be."[26]

For the Exploratorium, one such place to extend its reach was the San Francisco Civic Center. Funded by a multiyear grant from the National Science Foundation, Lani and the team from the Exploratorium developed *Middle Ground: Reconsidering Ourselves and Others*. The goal of the project is to bring together the city and the museum, using social science, to "create a lively and welcoming heart of the city."[27]

Working with the city, the team chose the steps leading to the library as the right place to build *Middle Ground*. There were plenty of people who passed through the civic center on any given day—commuters on their way to work, city and government officials, transients. The problem the team identified, however, is that the civic center wasn't so civic. People didn't stay. They didn't interact all that much. They passed through on their way from home to work, or from work to home, or between meetings. Rather than a gathering place, it served as a thoroughfare.

In their description of *Middle Ground*, the Exploratorium says, "We hope it's a place where people can drop their guard for a bit, enjoy the presence of others, and learn something new." So how can museums encourage the civic skill of gathering and social cohesion? How can we teach people, strangers even, how to work together?

The exhibit itself consists of fourteen bright yellow towers, each topped with a different sort of chair, everything from an office chair to a wheelchair, to reinforce the idea that it is okay to take a seat, talk together, and think about some of the issues they face as a community. The online publication Hoodline, which focuses on local content, described one such interaction

> One exhibit, Unseen Stories, asks visitors to share an experience during which they've been stereotyped, and one in which they believe they may have stereotyped someone.
>
> Exploratorium social scientist Heike Winterheld said the experience can be applicable right away, and could change someone's thought process or raise awareness of a topic that could otherwise feel outside of a single person's control.[28]

Another exhibit is called *Pulling Together*. In this exploration of how people work together, several ropes extend from a unit. Each person invites two or three others to pull with them. The experiment requires two attempts at pulling the ropes. On the first try, everyone pulls without knowing how hard they or the others are pulling. The second time, the screen shows how hard each person is pulling the rope. Lani explains, "When people can see their individual effort being tracked, they pull harder. It's a fascinating insight from science. We want to build in transparency of effort."

"We really value the term Civic Agency," says Lani. In showing people that their efforts matter, that their efforts can be important to a larger, collaborative effort, the museum can reinforce the idea that "I can make a difference in my community."

Lani says there are four keys to making this sort of public exhibit work.

1. **Freedom:** The space is somewhat ambiguous. You want those who visit and those who interact to do so in an environment where they feel free, and where they can exercise creative choices as they explore the interactions and conversation topics. If you want to teach civic agency, you must set up a situation where the public has agency in making choices.
2. **Rigor:** The Exploratorium is an institution grounded in science, and the exhibit itself is funded by the National Science Foundation (NSF), therefore, the science behind the exhibit must be rigorous. Thus, there is an independent evaluator from the NSF, data from people's responses is being collected throughout the duration of the exhibit and will be ana-

lyzed. The team is conducting exit interviews and tracking observations of behavior as folks interact. In short, the exhibit is both teaching and learning simultaneously.

3. **Reach:** The Exploratorium has more than 850,000 visitors each year.[29] San Francisco itself has just north of 880,000 residents, but more than twenty-five million tourists who visit each year. However, Lani estimates that 40 percent or so of the adult visitors to the Exploratorium have master's degrees, more than four times the national average. So by taking this exhibit to the streets, by having a museum presence beyond the walls of the museum, by existing in a public space, the museum is able to interact and connect with visitors who might never otherwise visit.

4. **Relevance:** By setting up in a public space, the museum takes on a different kind of relevance. For many visitors, a trip to the Exploratorium might take place once a year, once every few years, or once in a lifetime. By setting up shop in public spaces, and by having content that is available to anyone, the museum becomes a part of the daily lives of many. It becomes part of the fabric of their lives, the community, and the city.

The Exploratorium, by nature, encourages experimentation. One of the successful experiments that came out of *Middle Ground* is the "Pay It Forward Cafe." Prior to the installation of the exhibit, there was an Ethiopian family that operated a coffee cart near the entrance to the library. One of the evaluators for the program thought as part of the exhibit, they could build a basecamp for the coffee cart. What better way to foster conversation than to sit down over a hot cup of coffee? So they built a structure and encouraged an old Italian tradition. Those who had means would buy a cup of coffee for themselves, and purchase a token that someone else could use to get a cup of coffee for free. They used recycled mugs. The program was so successful that they often had to stop putting out the free tokens for coffee because so many people would purchase them. For those who couldn't afford to buy the coffee on their own, the token and the mug of coffee became "a passport for belonging." They could sit down and enjoy a cup of coffee just like anyone else.

One of the problems in densely populated cities, says Lani, is that "empathy starts to fail." People often want to help others and want to connect with those around them, but the problems can appear overwhelming. A passerby might want to share some spare change to buy a meal for someone in need, but when there are hundreds, or thousands in such a situation, it is too much for a well-intentioned commuter to take on. *Middle Ground* offers a possible solution. On one hand, it gives people a way of better dealing in the immediate, but it also helps to illustrate underlying systemic problems.

Doing work like this isn't easy though. Lani cautions that you can't just do something like *Middle Ground* anywhere. "Just like you can't farm by throwing seeds out a window," he says. Institutions need to be incredibly intentional and thoughtful about finding both the right partners and the right place to bring folks together.

Even when you have the right partner and the right place, there can still be incredible challenges. The museum exhibit development process doesn't always work easily with the city permitting process. "It is tough to build an exhibit and get approval for it through city channels at the same time," says Lani. But the payoff can be remarkable for both the institution and the community.

"There is something remarkable about working in a public space," says Lani, "It's like creating a front porch for your efforts. It's like inviting the world to sit on your front porch. You get a lot more eyes on your institution." The Exploratorium, through their work in public spaces, is embracing the idea of civic agency. Lani says the goal is to "offer a broad spectrum of offerings to the general public. We don't just want to create 'Wow' exhibitions. We really want to create spaces that people are enticed to be involved with."

For Lani, this civic work has become a personal passion as well. "The more I get into this, the more I just want people to be civil to one another," he says. "Ultimately, our relationships are more important than our politics, and I am a cheerleader for helping people get past those dumb traps of being manipulated."

Middle Ground was designed with the express intention of bringing people together. "People are desperate to talk together, to play together, to interact with one another," says Lani. And in a world increasingly disconnected, divided, and polarized, perhaps it is museums that can help bring them back together.

Table 4.1. Museum Profile: The Exploratorium

Location	San Francisco, CA
Type of Museum	Public Learning Laboratory
Annual Visitors	~390,000 (2019)
Staff	252 full-time 183 part-time 203 high school explainers 231 volunteers 14 interns
Budget	$45 million (2018)
Collection	Hundreds of explore-for-yourself exhibits, a website with more than 35,000 pages of content, film screenings, evening art and science events for adults, plus much more

Information from https://www.exploratorium.edu/about/fact-sheet

SIMI VALLEY, CALIFORNIA: UNDERSTANDING BOTH SIDES

Simi Valley is located in Ventura County, California. Depending on traffic, Simi Valley is anywhere from thirty minutes to three hours away from Los Angeles. If you exit Olsen Road and make a left up Presidential Drive, you'll take a winding road past banners of every president ever to have served the United States. About halfway up the road, just as you approach Abraham Lincoln, you can see the majestic Wood Ranch Reservoir in the distance. At the top of the hill, at 40 Presidential Drive, with a view that on a clear day stretches to the Pacific Ocean and the Channel Islands, sits the Ronald Reagan Presidential Library and Museum. President Reagan was fond of quoting John Winthrop's "shining city on a hill" in his descriptions of the promise of America. His library sits at the top of just such a hill.

In 2011, during the centennial celebration of his birth, the Reagan Foundation, the nonprofit formed by the president himself, raised millions of dollars to update the museum and launch an education center dedicated to cultivating the next generation of citizen-leaders. He believed that the connection between education and democracy went back to the very founding of the country. Ben Franklin, elder statesman at the Constitutional Convention—the very same man who pronounced we had "a republic, if we could keep it"—did his part to keep it by starting the University of Pennsylvania. Thomas Jefferson, third president, author of the Declaration of Independence, also started a university—the University of Virginia.

Teaching students about American history, and helping them learn civic skills, has been at the core of the education work done at the Reagan Foundation for much of the past decade. And a civic skill that has taken on ever more importance with each passing year is information and media literacy.

A June 2018 study by the Pew Research Center reveals that in a fast-paced, social media, information superhighway world, the ability of Americans to correctly discern the difference between fact and opinion is only slightly better than a random guess. "The main portion of the study, which measured the public's ability to distinguish between five factual statements and five opinion statements, found that a majority of Americans correctly identified at least three of the five statements in each set."[30] As a former teacher, I take no solace in knowing that the majority of Americans earned a D− on the difference between facts and opinions.

In a digital age, the ability to quickly sort through an endless stream of content from multiple sources of information, and make determinations about the value of that information, is absolutely essential. The study further goes on to point out that this ability to distinguish between fact and opinion gets even worse when the information appeals to a particular political viewpoint. "Overall, Republicans and Democrats were more likely to clas-sify both factual *and* opinion statements as factual when they appealed most to their side."[31] Essentially, both Democrats and Republicans are more likely to believe information as fact if it supports their previously held be-liefs. Anything that contradicts this partisan belief, even if it is factual, is dismissed out of hand as "fake news."

Part of the reason we can't have productive political discussions is that each side has their own set of facts from their own trusted sources of news and, as a result, there is not common ground for a discussion to even begin. Whereas the Museum of Art at the University of New Hampshire is leverag-ing its collection and its role in the broader university community to teach the civic skill of having tough dialogues, and the Exploratorium is applying the methodology of experiential learning to teach folks about what it means to come together as a community, the Ronald Reagan Presidential Foundation and Institute is leveraging the story of "The Great Communicator" to teach students how to gather, sort, and best utilize facts in a national civil debate competition. Whereas a typical politically minded citizen might look for facts to build on a previously held belief or articles from familiar news sources that reinforce a particular ideology, debate encourages participants to cobble together compelling arguments on both sides of an issue.

Originally launched to coincide with the 2012 presidential election, the Ronald Reagan Great Communicator Debate Series "was founded to de-velop engaged, informed, and conscientious citizen-leaders by hosting a national series of high school debates. The debates search for students who can effectively use logic, evidence, and personality to communicate their ideas. . . . Engaging in civil discourse is a hallmark of American democracy, and this debate series encourages [students] to join the conversation on is-sues our country faces."[32]

For the sake of transparency, I worked with a dedicated team of educators and partners around the country to create this program so, from here on out, I will use "we" to describe the many contributors whose passion for the role of speech and debate in democracy has made this a meaningful program for students and educators alike.

We originally developed the program hoping to capture the wave of pow-erful civic engagement that accompanies a presidential election. Having worked behind the scenes as the Ronald Regan Presidential Library hosted a GOP primary debate in 2011, one that millions of viewers from around the world tuned into, we wanted to both develop and highlight effective commu-nication skills for students across the country.

Critical for our team was ensuring that a communication skill competition was nonpartisan. Effectively harnessing the tools of communication is an incredibly important civic skill because if a citizen, a member of a community, has the ability to communicate, that citizen has the ability to bring about positive change and inspire others.

At the Ronald Reagan Presidential Foundation and Institute, it is our mission to work with students from around the country to take that power and that responsibility seriously; to cultivate the next generation of thoughtful, informed, and engaged citizens and leaders; and to help develop the very sort of young leaders up to the task of "keeping" our republic.

Speech and debate is, for my money, the best activity a student can engage in to become a guardian of democracy. Debaters, to be effective, must know their history and must be well versed in their facts; they know the issues, and they can communicate about them successfully and impactfully.

One of my favorite parts of competitive speech and debate is that students are fully prepared to debate **both** sides of the issue. When we conduct our national championship round, the student does not even know which side he or she will be advocating for until a flip of the coin just a few minutes before the round begins. So well versed in the topic are they that they can literally take either side of the debate. Some of our national champions have argued for an idea in a semifinal round, and then against the same idea in the final round.

Figure 4.7. Katie Kleinle competes at the Reagan Library in the national championship of the Great Communicator Debate Series

Photo courtesy of the Ronald Reagan Presidential Foundation and Institute

In fact, I think many of our politicians today could learn a thing or two from the students who participate in speech and debate programs about what it means to fully understand an issue.

Table 4.2. Museum Profile: Ronald Reagan Presidential Foundation and Institute

Location	Simi Valley, CA and Washington, DC
Type of Museum	Presidential Library and Museum
Annual Visitors	~390,000 (2019)
Staff *Numbers here represent the nonprofit foundation and do not include the federal employees of the National Archives*	49 full-time 63 part-time 400+ volunteers 8 interns
Budget	~$25 million (2018)
Collection	55 million+ presidential documents, photos, videos, and physical objects (including Air Force One, Marine One) from the Reagan presidency

LESSONS LEARNED

In order to cultivate important civic skills, there are several lessons learned in this chapter that can be emulated at any museum, regardless of focus, size, budget, or staff bandwidth.

1. **Partnerships:** At the Reagan Foundation, our vision for the debate series is to inspire the next generation of civic-minded leaders and to hone their ability to communicate powerfully on important issues. Though we have archival videos of presidential debates, and some ideas about what makes for successful civic and political communication, we had no experience in the formalized world of academic debate. We reached out to the National Speech and Debate Association, the largest organization of middle and high school speech and debate students. In 1969, they reached three hundred thousand members. In 2000, they celebrated one million members. They have been the leading organization in the space since 1925. Luckily for us, they were willing to support our fledgling enterprise and advised and consulted us as we developed the program. Shawn Lani and the team at the Exploratorium worked with the City of San Francisco, the Civic Center, the family that owned the coffee cart, and many others to bring *Middle Ground* to life. Kristina Durocher and the Museum of Art worked with the Civil Discourse Lab, the University of New Hampshire, student volunteers and organizations, For Freedoms,

and others to create better dialogue and raise awareness of freedom on campus. In short, to build civic skills and to do civic work, you must practice what you preach. If you want to teach visitors and the public how to work together effectively, you must model it by working effectively with others.

2. **Extend the Front Porch:** As Shawn Lani so eloquently stated about the work of the Exploratorium, it is important to extend the front porch. Just as you must work with others, you must make the museum an institution that exists in the fabric of a community rather than a building that is placed in a community. At the Museum of Art, they planted yard signs near walkways on campus; they worked with other departments. They will work with a local community college to extend the program. At the Reagan Foundation, we wanted to extend our reach, so we partnered with speech and debate regional leaders in Washington, DC, New York, Texas, California, and Missouri to host regional competitions. With a few banner bugs and some dedicated staff, we worked with partners across the country to have a presence and to encourage information literacy and communication skills. Having access to the competition was incredibly important for us as well. For students who were unable to travel to one of our regions, we hosted an online competition where students debated over the internet.

3. **Support for Success:** At the Museum of Art and the Civil Discourse Lab, students are empowered to be community discussion facilitators with hours of training and practice, and discussion guides help ensure they are successful. The Exploratorium team built a coffee stand to encourage the community to sit and chat, and lent their interactive exhibition expertise to refresh a decaying civic space. At the Reagan Foundation, each year our team chooses a debate topic. In order to make sure students can prepare for success in the tournament, we offer a number of online resources. We post videos of past national championships so students can see what this form of debate looks like at the highest level. We have created how-to videos complete with clips from our archives so that students know exactly what the judges are looking for. We also work to provide all competitors with an initial set of resources from vetted sources. In the past we've partnered with ProCon.org, one of the nation's leading sources of nonpartisan research on controversial topics, to ensure that students have compelling sources as they prepare for their debates.

4. **Ultimately, It's About Community:** For our competition at the Reagan Foundation, we invite the top two qualifiers from each region to our national championship. A total of sixteen students, their coaches, and families join the group. The final round is held in our Air Force One Pavilion,

the same space that has housed several presidential primary debates. The students debate in the same space as men and women who have vied for the highest office in the land. The stakes are big. We offer a total of $50,000 in college scholarship money to our competitors. The national champion takes home $10,000. Even though what brings these students together is the competition, and there are significant incentives for them to compete fiercely, our museum does not emphasize the competition. Instead, we invite the competitors to get to know one another. We eat meals together, tour the museum, invite guest speakers to address the group on themes of leadership and communication, and encourage alumni of the program to come back and offer tips for success. Coach Jack Tuckness of Central High School in Springfield, Missouri, who has taught speech and debate for twenty years and was, in 2018, inducted into the National Speech and Debate Association Hall of Fame, says that this spirit of community makes our competition unique. The museum is "able to create an atmosphere that allows the contestants to become friends before they meet as competitors."[33] In this way, we hope to create a generation of passionate leaders who care more about people and finding common ground than zero-sum ideology. The Exploratorium invites strangers to work together to pull a rope, and encourages those with means to pay it forward for a cup of coffee. The Museum of Art brings together folks with diverse viewpoints and teaches them how to have a productive conversation.

These are just a few examples of the remarkable work museums across the country are doing to develop civic skills. Ford's Theatre, for example, has an amazing oratory program that leverages the legacy of Abraham Lincoln to teach communication. Having students engage in democratic simulations is also key, and there are a number of institutions across the country that have students role-play including, but not limited to, the Edward M. Kennedy Institute for the US Senate in Boston; the Harry S Truman Library in Independence, Missouri; and the Magic House, a children's museum where kindergarteners simulate the legislative process, in St. Louis.

Outside of a museum, the world is often driven by what divides us. Our social media feeds, our choice of news sources, where we live, what sort of car we might drive, or the party we choose when registering to vote makes up just a tiny fraction of who we are, what we believe, and how we exist in this world. Inside of a museum, or as we approach the extended front porch of a museum, this changes. We share a common experience, we learn together, we eat together, we read label copy or take in an exhibit together, we pull ropes together and then pull harder when we realize that we need to. And sometimes, we offer a cup of coffee to someone in need. We don't stop to ask what political party they belong to, who they voted for, or what they think about the political issue of the day. We offer the cup of coffee, and we accept the cup of coffee because sometimes coffee is more than coffee. It's a passport, an invitation, a reason to be somewhere and to feel like you deserve to be there—to feel a part of something bigger and more important, to belong.

NOTES

1. "NH at-a-Glance." 2019. State Constitution—Bill of Rights." NG.gov. Accessed October 11, 2019. https://www.nh.gov/glance/bill-of-rights.htm.

2. Benenson, Bob. 2007. "A History of U.S. Presidential Primaries: 1912–64." CQ Politics, December 25, 2007. https://web.archive.org/web/20071228132247/http:/www.cqpolitics.com/wmspage.cfm?docid=news-000002649356.

3. Mayer, William G., ed. 2004. *The Making of the Presidential Candidates 2004.* Lanham, MD: Rowman & Littlefield.

4. McDermott, Casey. 2019. "Dixville Notch's 'First In The Nation' Midnight Voting Tradition May End Over Election Rules." WBUR News. NHPR-WBUR, February 13, 2019. https://www.wbur.org/news/2019/02/13/dixville-notchs-first-in-the-nation-midnight-voting-tradition-may-end-over-election-rules.

5. DeSilver, Drew. 2018. "U.S. Trails Most Developed Countries in Voter Turnout." Pew Research Center, May 21, 2018. https://www.pewresearch.org/fact-tank/2018/05/21/u-s-voter-turnout-trails-most-developed-countries/.

6. Gould, Jonathan, Kathleen Hall Jamieson, Peter Levine, Ted McConnell, and David B. Smith, eds. 2011. *Guardian of Democracy: The Civic Mission of Schools.* Philadelphia: Leonore Annenberg Institute for Civics of the Annenberg Public Policy Center at the University of Pennsylvania.

7. United States Elections Project. 2018. "2016 November General Election Turnout Rates." Electproject, September 5, 2018. http://www.electproject.org/2016g.

8. "Government of New Hampshire." Wikipedia. Accessed January 6, 2020. https://en.wikipedia.org/wiki/Government_of_New_Hampshire.

9. Quoted from a phone interview between Kristina Durocher and the author.

10. American Psychological Association and stressinamerica.org. 2017. "Stress in America: The State of Our Nation." American Psychological Association. https://www.apa.org/news/press/releases/stress/2017/state-nation.pdf.

11. "More Now Say It's 'Stressful' to Discuss Politics With People They Disagree With." 2018. Pew Research Center. *U.S. Politics & Policy*, November 5, 2018. https://www.people-press.org/2018/11/05/more-now-say-its-stressful-to-discuss-politics-with-people-they-disagree-with/.

12. Underwood, Katherine. 2017. "University of New Hampshire Group Calls for Change After Cinco de Mayo Celebration." NBC10 Boston, May 10, 2017. https://www.nbcboston.com/news/local/university-of-new-hampshire-group-calls-for-change-after-cinco-de-mayo-celebration/18089/.

13. Stelter, Jessie. 2018. "Civil Discourse Lab Aims to Give Students Outlet for Discussion." *The New Hampshire*, December 6, 2018. https://tnhdigital.com/2018/12/06/civil-discourse-lab-aims-to-give-students-outlet-for-discussion/.

14. Heath, Renee. 2018. "Civil Discourse Lab: End of the Year Report May 2018." University of New Hampshire, Department of Communication, May 2018. https://mypages.unh.edu/sites/default/files/ne-arctic-convergence/files/cdl_end_of_the_year_final.pdf.

15. Aldredge, Michelle. 2019. "Yoav Horesh: Aftermath." ArtNewEngland. Accessed November 1, 2019. http://artnewengland.com/ed_review/yoav-horesh-aftermath/.

16. Aldredge. 2019. "Yoav Horesh: Aftermath."

17. "For Freedoms." For Freedoms. Accessed November 6, 2019. https://forfreedoms.org/.

18. "Explore." For Freedoms. Accessed November 6, 2019. https://forfreedoms.org/explore/.

19. Cogswell, Ned. 2016. "The History of The Hippie Cultural Movement." Culture Trip, May 16, 2016. https://theculturetrip.com/north-america/usa/california/articles/the-history-of-the-hippie-cultural-movement/.

20. Leip, David. 2019. "2016 Presidential General Election Results." Dave Leip's Atlas of U.S. Elections. Accessed November 6, 2019. https://uselectionatlas.org/RESULTS/.

21. Knight, Heather. 2019. "SF's Homelessness Crisis Crash-Lands on One Tiny Street." SFChronicle.com. *San Francisco Chronicle*, October 1, 2019. https://www.sfchronicle.com/bayarea/heatherknight/article/Sidewalk-boulder-battle-as-emblem-of-city-s-14481396.php.

22. Knight. 2019. "SF's Homelessness Crisis."

23. Gurian. 2007. *Civilizing the Museum*, 48.

24. "Exploratorium." Wikipedia. Accessed February 21, 2020. https://en.wikipedia.org/wiki/Exploratorium.

25. Rothstein, Edward. 2013. "An Emphasis on Newton's Laws (and a Little Lawlessness)." *New York Times*, April 16, 2013. https://www.nytimes.com/2013/04/17/arts/design/the-new-exploratorium-opens-in-san-francisco.html?pagewanted=all&_r=0.

26. Quoted from a phone interview between Shawn Lani and the author.

27. *Middle Ground: Reconsidering Ourselves and Others*. 2019. Exploratorium, October 1, 2019. https://www.exploratorium.edu/middleground/.

28. Sisto, Carrie. 2019. "New Exploratorium Exhibit in Civic Center Invites Visitors to 'Pull up a Chair' and Chat." Hoodline, July 26, 2019. https://hoodline.com/2019/07/new-exploratorium-exhibit-in-civic-center-invites-visitors-to-pull-up-a-chair-and-chat.

29. "Exploratorium Fact Sheet." 2019. Exploratorium, August 28, 2019. https://www.exploratorium.edu/about/fact-sheet.

30. Mitchell, Amy, Jeffrey Gottfried, Michael Barthel, and Nami Sumida. 2018. "Distinguishing Between Factual and Opinion Statements in the News." Pew Research Center. Journalism and Media, June 18, 2018. https://www.journalism.org/2018/06/18/distinguishing-between-factual-and-opinion-statements-in-the-news/.

31. Mitchell et al. 2018. "Distinguishing Between Factual and Opinion."

32. "Great Communicator Debate Series." 2019. Ronald Reagan Presidential Foundation & Institute. Accessed November 9, 2019. https://www.reaganfoundation.org/education/scholarship-programs/great-communicator-debate-series/.

33. Quoted from an email correspondence between Jack Tuckness and the author.

5

Putting It All Together: Civic Action

Civic participation over a lifetime, working in neighborhoods and communities and service of all kinds—military and civilian, full-time and part-time, national and international—will strengthen America's civic purpose.

—John McCain

We are here also because of our love for democracy, because of our deep-seated belief that democracy transformed from thin paper to thick action is the greatest form of government on earth.

—Dr. Martin Luther King Jr.

Though most of my elementary school science lessons have long since receded into the dusty, unused, storage shelves of my memory, there is one lesson that comes to mind as I contemplate museums and civic action.

In physics, potential energy is "the energy held by an object because of its position relative to other objects, stresses within itself, its electric charge, or other factors."[1] I vividly remember our teacher invited us to sit in a half circle on the carpet at the front of the classroom. On the table she had set up a ramp. She reached into the pocket of her thick wool sweater and removed one of those brightly colored bouncing balls.

"When I place the ball here," she said as she positioned it at the top of the ramp, "it has *potential energy*. It isn't moving yet, but it has the *potential* to move very quickly.

"What do you suppose would happen," she asked, "if one of you were to give it just the slightest little nudge toward the ramp?"

This moment of anticipation—*What do you suppose would happen?*—is precisely where we find ourselves in our exploration of the civic mission of museums. Let's return to John Cotton Dana. In the opening chapter we explored the idea that most important of all the essential work of museums is "such activities as may fairly be supposed to produce beneficial effects on their respective communities." I want to return to that idea now because in many ways the previous chapters of this book have been all about *potential civic energy*.

A ball at the top of a ramp has potential energy because of:

1. Its position—it sits at the top of an incline.
2. The force of gravity pulling it down toward the earth.
3. Its shape—the roundness of the ball means that even the slightest exertion of force will send the ball moving.
4. Its weight—because the ball is relatively light, there is not much force required to initiate movement.
5. The intent of the teacher—she wants to demonstrate how potential energy shifts to kinetic energy.

Now consider a visitor to your museum, or a member of your community, or a student participating in a museum program. To this point, this book has explored all the ways in which museums create an environment of potential civic energy. Museums define, collect, cocreate, and share civic knowledge, but civic knowledge can be transmitted from an institution to an individual without *producing* any beneficial effect on a community. It can be akin to taking a file from one hard drive and transferring it to another. Let's call this the *Jeopardy* effect. On the TV game show *Jeopardy*, contestants compete to display their mastery of a wide array of categorized trivia. On the specific environment of the show, this knowledge can lead to prize money. Any knowledge that has been accumulated over the course of a lifetime—through school, museums, pop culture, reading, etc.—has the *potential* to be useful on the show, and has the *potential* to produce a beneficial effect for the person who possesses the knowledge (and can both access that knowledge and hit the buzzer before the other competitors). However, possessing the knowledge in and of itself doesn't necessarily lead to a beneficial effect. You have probably heard the saying, "*Knowledge is power.*" This is certainly true—however, it is an outlet. An outlet in your home is a tremendous source of power, but if you don't plug something into the outlet, that power goes unused. It is untapped.

In a museum, sometimes our exhibits and tours are designed this way. We present an exhibit, and within the exhibit are fifty carefully curated facts, descriptions, or pieces of pertinent information and context about the exhibit. Through label copy and interpretation, the visitor has the potential to now be in possession of fifty facts. The visitor has knowledge. They have power. But when they leave the museum, the stickiness factor of that knowledge might not be very high. They hop into their car or onto public transportation, pull out their cell phone, and a tsunami of new content—social media, work, news updates—means that the knowledge they gained in the museum might disappear well before it gets written to the brain's long-term memory. Hence, even if they were to appear on *Jeopardy*, and the topic happened to be about the content from your museum exhibit, they might not remember. Really, if they walk out the door of the museum and don't put that knowledge to use, it doesn't mean much.

The same is true for civic mindset and skillset. If someone is mentally prepared for their role as a citizen, but never actually votes, participates in a public discussion, advocates for a cause, campaigns for a candidate, or contributes to their community, does that mental preparation mean much? If someone is a talented public speaker, who never speaks publicly or has the skills to contribute to community building but opts to spend their days on the couch watching movies or is an expert at facilitating conversations around difficult political topics but prefers to read quietly by the fire—are any of these important skills civically useful?

What I argue for here is not the importance of civic action or civic engagement above and beyond knowledge, mindset, and skillset. For the same reason, I wouldn't advocate for using a vacuum cleaner separately from a wall outlet. The greatest benefit is produced when these disparate elements are woven together. A vacuum only works when it is properly connected to an outlet. There is an interconnectedness between knowledge, mindset, skills, and action, and museums are at their best when they can effectively connect knowledge to action, the past to the present, and serve as a gathering place for diverse individuals and groups from the community.

So, what is **civic action**? According to the 2010 version of the *International Encyclopedia of Civil Society*, "Though widely diffused the concept of civic action is not clearly defined, nor has it a well-established meaning. For example, civic action is referred to enabling people to make sure legislators hear their voices; to building knowledge on important issues and take action through campaigns to change the behavior of public and private institutions; to citizens becoming more active members in their community; up to a military force operating in favor of civilians including dental, engineering, medical, veterinarian activities.

"Civic action neither has a precise placing in scientific community. References to this concept can indeed be found in the literature on collective action and social movements, on participatory democracy, on advocacy, on political participation, on community organizing, on social networks, on social capital, on direct democracy, on volunteerism, on stakeholder theory, etc."[2] So it is difficult to offer a simple and concise definition of civic action because there is an incredibly wide array of ways in which the term can be (and has been) used. For the purposes of this work, I'll attempt to embrace the broad spirit of the term. Civic action, for museums, can be any action, taken by a museum, its trustees or staff, its visitors, or those it encounters on its extended "front porch," that serves to produce that beneficial effect in the community that was key to Dana. Civic action over time, or a sustained series of civic actions, we'll call civic engagement.

The 2000 book *Civic Responsibility and Higher Education* offers this description of civic engagement, "Civic engagement means working to make a difference in the civic life of our communities and developing the combination of knowledge, skills, values and motivation to make that difference. It means promoting the quality of life in a community, through both political and nonpolitical processes."[3] You will no doubt note the similarity in language and thinking to Dana's definition of museums doing their best work. "Promoting the quality of life in a community" and producing a beneficial effect in the community are nearly identical descriptors—one of civic engagement and one of the essential work of museums. One could argue that these are one and the same.

In 2013, a group of "fifteen professional organizations committed to the advancement of social studies education"[4] produced what has come to be known as the "C3 Framework." Recent education reform efforts have led to a great deal of focus on the need to prepare students for success in higher education and in the workforce, or, more simply, college and career. As federal funding and state requirements for social studies instruction and civic learning have fallen to historic lows, advocates for the importance of civic learning have argued that a third "C" should be added to college and career: civic life. Long before students head off to college, they should be engaged and active citizens, and research shows that some of the most active citizens in terms of voting and giving back to their communities are those who have retired from their careers. This argument, that our nation's youngsters need to be prepared for civic life just as urgently as college and career, led to the creation of the "C3 Framework." Organizations including the American Bar Association, the American Historical Association, National History Day, and many others collaborated to produce the framework which is a guide for how to prepare students for civic life. The framework has four dimensions. I'll explain the first three very briefly only for the larger context.

Dimension 1: Developing Questions and Planning Inquiries. For students to learn, they need to be able to ask and explore "compelling questions."

Dimension 2: Applying Disciplinary Concepts and Tools. Here, learners apply the concepts and tools of civics, history, geography, and economics to explore their compelling questions.

Dimension 3: Evaluating Sources and Using Evidence. As learners explore their questions, they should draw on reliable primary and secondary source material from archives, museums, books, video, etc., as they prepare to respond to their compelling questions.

Dimension 4: Communicating Conclusions and Taking Informed Action. Essentially, now that we have gathered knowledge from reliable sources, used our minds and our disciplinary skills to evaluate this information—what do we do with it? What benefit can we produce?

In some ways, this is a radical approach to civic learning. It suggests that merely knowing the information is not an acceptable end. Multiple choice tests, or knowing the right definitions of key terms, is only a small part of the process. In the "C3 Framework," you must, like Dana suggests, be able to produce something—a learner must act. In the process of *producing* something, they also *become* something—an engaged citizen.

Active and responsible citizens identify and analyze public problems; deliberate with other people about how to define and address issues; take constructive, collaborative action; reflect on their actions; create and sustain groups; and influence institutions both large and small. They vote, serve on juries, follow the news and current events, and participate in voluntary groups and efforts. Teaching students to act in these ways—as citizens—significantly enhances preparation for college and career. Many of the same skills that are needed for active and responsible citizenship—working effectively with other people, deliberating and reasoning quantitatively about issues, following the news, and forming and sustaining groups—are also crucial to success in the twenty-first-century workplace and in college. Individual mastery of content often no longer suffices; students should also develop the capacity to work together to apply knowledge to real problems.[5]

How then can museums leverage their assets, collections, and abilities to cultivate civic mindset and skill sets into the ability to work with students, visitors, and their communities to "take informed action?"

VOTING

In terms of civic action, voting is far and away the most common form of political engagement. According to the 2010 *Civic Life in America: Key Findings on the Civic Health of the Nation* report, 57.1 percent[6] of those who are voting age cast a vote in the 2008 presidential election. Though one could argue that a voting rate of 57.1 percent is nothing to be proud of, other measures of civic participation rank much lower, as you can see in table 5.1.

Table 5.1. National Percentages of Various Forms of Civic Participation (2010)

Category	National Percentage
Voting (2008 election)	57.1%
Occasionally exchanging favors with neighbors	41.3%
Participating in one or more groups (civic, school, sports, religious)	35.1%
Volunteering with an organization	26.5%
Contacted public officials to express opinion	10.3%

Acknowledging a host of issues around access to the ballot—including but not limited to: voter ID laws; purges of voting rolls; access to polling stations for rural, elderly, or socioeconomically disadvantaged voters; a plethora of misinformation around candidates and ballot measures; election fraud; inconsistent or confusing ballot design—that I do not intend to explore at length here, voting is, arguably, the broadest and simplest form of civic action. Voting, by the numbers, is the most common form of civic action in the country.

Research shows that not only is voting the most common form of civic action, it is also a gateway to other forms of civic action. People who vote volunteer 23 percent more often than those who do not, attend public meetings roughly 24 percent more frequently, and exchange favors with their neighbors more than 20 percent more often. So, for museums who want to encourage civic action and civic engagement, one way to get started is to offer your museum as a polling place.

In an October 2018 article in *Smithsonian Magazine*, Charles Hyde, president and CEO of the Benjamin Harrison Presidential Site in Indianapolis, Indiana, offered five reasons for why museums should serve as polling places:

1. **Awareness:** As a place where communities already convene, museums tend to have higher awareness levels than public service locations like a police station or a church.
2. **Accessibility:** Museums tend to already be ADA-compliant and optimized to welcome diverse audiences.
3. **Mutual benefit:** Museums can demonstrate their commitment to equity, accessibility, and nonpartisan civic engagement without a significant cost to their bottom line.
4. **Lead by example:** Want good citizens in your community? Model good civic behavior. No one is satisfied today with the injunction to "do as I say, not as I do."
5. **Call to action:** A federal judge once told me that as a presidential site, we have special permission, if not a special obligation, to call people to their civic duty. The charge applies to all of us as educational organiza-

tions, whether our day-to-day work engages us in art, science, or the humanities. Civics is central to all disciplines in the end. Serving as a polling site is one of many expressions of civic leadership on a spectrum of engagement we seek to foster.[7]

Hyde's list serves as a great checklist for making the case for why your museum should serve as a polling site. In addition, it sends a message to your community—our museum is not just a place to visit once, it really is a thriving hub for this community. It is a place for us to gather and conduct the business of the community at large. Not to mention, hosting a polling station might bring members of your community in that have not previously visited. In short, it can be a win for the community and for the museum. Hyde also worked with the Indiana University and Purdue University Indianapolis (IUPUI) School for Public and Environmental Affairs to study the impact of having the museum serve as a polling place. "Most dramatically, the museum's precinct in 2016 outperformed citywide turnout by six percentage points, compared to the prior presidential election cycle, when the precinct's voting trailed citywide numbers by more than two percentage points,"[8] he wrote. Though they are still delving into better understanding the reasons behind the 8-point swing in voter turnout, the initial results suggest that serving as a polling place can be a win for democracy too. If your museum can bring a new visitor or member of the community to your institution to perform the civic action of casting a vote, you have a better chance of working with them long term to promote civic engagement. One vote becomes many votes, and if someone is interested in casting a ballot, they might be more inclined to participate in a public discussion.

Table 5.2. Museum Profile: Benjamin Harrison Presidential Site

Location	Indianapolis, IN
Type of Museum	Presidential site, Historic Home
Annual Visitors	29,000+
Staff	14 staff
	163 volunteers
Budget	$914,457 (2017)
Collection	10,000 photographs, furniture, art, documents, and campaign and presidency artifacts in the collection

HOSTING PUBLIC MEETINGS

In the chapter on civic skillset, we mentioned a few of the museums that have hosted presidential primary debates, a high-profile form of a gathering centered around public and political affairs. While not every museum will have the opportunity or even the space to host such a gathering, museums can, do, and should host public and community gatherings. These meetings could include everything from local associations like the Rotary, Kiwanis, American Legion, or Chamber of Commerce, to debates between candidates for local office, town hall–type gatherings for officials at the local, state, and/or national level, or hosting tours or receptions for gatherings of state, regional, or national organizations.

At our museum, we work with the local youth council, a youth advisory group to the city council, to host a Youth Town Hall each year. The students identify the topic or topics they'd like to address; we then work with them to issue invitations to panelists from the school district, the city, the county, the state legislature, and the US Congress to participate. The students conduct research on the issues, audition for the roles of speakers, moderators, campus guides for the speakers, or social media moderators, and do all of the preparation for the event. For us, it is key that the students have agency in the design and running of the Town Hall. Officials are aware of the general topics to be covered, but not given the specific questions ahead of time. More than four hundred students from local schools are invited to be in the audience for the Town Hall. They are allowed to submit questions via text and social

Figure 5.1.   Students from the Simi Youth Council interview community leaders as part of a Simi Youth Town Hall focused on substance abuse and teens
Photo courtesy of the Ronald Reagan Presidential Foundation and Institute

media. Questions are then screened and chosen by student moderators. Students are encouraged by the teachers and the students on the youth council to ask tough, but respectful, questions. What results is a substantial policy discussion being hosted by students who, in many cases, aren't yet old enough to vote. This doesn't mean that every question is a cutting policy question. They are kids after all. During one Town Hall, a student submitted a question online, "Pancakes or Waffles?" Each panelist answered thoughtfully and shared a story on why they preferred pancakes or waffles, but the chief of police brought down the house with his one-word response: Donuts.

This is one of our favorite partnerships. The youth council contributes motivated students who prepare themselves well to run a Town Hall. We provide space, our reputation within the community as a convener, and training for the students on stage presence and preparation. The school district sends students and teachers who are interested in learning how to be civically engaged, and the elected and appointed officials enjoy engaging with some of their youngest constituents around substantial issues.

The Pioneer City County Museum in Sweetwater, Texas, is different than the Reagan Library in Simi Valley, California. Whereas the Reagan Foundation has roughly thirty staff and several million dollars dedicated to education work alone, the Pioneer City County Museum has one full-time staff member, one part-timer who comes in from 1 p.m. to 4 p.m. Tuesdays through Fridays, and an operating budget of less than $100,000. Whereas the city of Simi Valley has a population of more than 120,000 people[9] and is situated less than an hour from Los Angeles, one of the largest metropolitan areas in the country, Sweetwater, Texas, has a population of just over 10,000[10] and a county population of roughly 16,000. Despite these differences in staff, budget, and population, the Sweetwater Pioneer City County Museum, situated in the historic Ragland House, also plays a crucial role in creating opportunities for civic action. In fact, the museum served as a convener for a county-wide summit that brought together a number of different sectors to better focus on the needs and assets of the community. This included folks from local government, the healthcare industry, the school system, and local religious institutions. The summit resulted in a wide-ranging report that was submitted to the city and county. They also interviewed candidates for the local sheriff's election and posted the interviews so that the local voters would be better informed when making their selection come Election Day.

There is no shortage of ways museums can leverage their facilities and resources to host or cohost public meetings. If your visitors and community are interested in the events and issues that consume the present, they might be inclined to explore the deeper context and history of some of these civic issues.

Table 5.3. Museum Profile: Pioneer City County Museum

Location	Sweetwater, TX
Type of Museum	Historic Home
Annual Visitors	1,300 visitors, plus other attendees at public events
Staff	1 full-time
	1 part-time
Budget	$72,000 (2019)
Collection	Artifacts and photographs that preserve the history and share the culture of Sweetwater and Nolan County

EXPLORING HISTORIC AND CURRENT EVENTS

In a city known for some of the largest and most visited museums in the country, President Lincoln's Cottage, is a hidden gem. Located less than five miles from the White House or the Smithsonian National Museum of American History, Lincoln's Cottage sits to the northeast of downtown Washington, DC; with roughly thirty thousand visitors annually, it sees just a fraction of the visitors other DC institutions receive. That said, the impact of this place, both historically and in the present day, reverberates across the country and around the world.

Historically speaking, President Lincoln spent more than one-quarter of his presidency in residence at what was then called the Old Soldiers' Home. He would ride via horseback between the "cottage" and the White House during the Civil War. Their motto is that President Lincoln's Cottage is "a home for brave ideas." This is true historically—Lincoln composed the Emancipation Proclamation (arguably one of the single most important documents in the history of the United States) while at the cottage—but it is also an invocation to the next generation of brave thinkers. The cottage itself allows plenty of space for those brave ideas. The rooms of the cottage are largely empty, and the room where Lincoln composed the Emancipation Proclamation is largely bare, except for a small desk that sits by the window.

In a post about the sort of experience they hoped to create for visitors at the cottage, CEO Erin Carlson Mast wrote, "We chose to create a 'Museum of Ideas' using a conversational, guided-tour approach, rather than a museum of things with a traditional 'velvet rope' lecture-style tour."[11] What results for visitors is what she describes as the *Lincoln shiver.* "The shiver is a feeling one gets just by being in the Cottage—or on the grounds—here at the Soldiers' Home, on a hilltop in northwest Washington, DC. The shiver came at different times for different people. For some, it was when they rested their hand on the banister and walked up the same steps as Lincoln.

For others, it came when they heard a story of what happened here. Still others felt the shiver after the fact—realizing the enormity of what Lincoln grappled with here during the Civil War." In some ways that shiver represents the physical impact of what happens when museums are successfully able to forge a connection between the past they represent and the modern world. The shiver comes as modern visitors feel the ripple effects of Lincoln's Emancipation Proclamation, and realize how much his brave idea altered the course of American history.

That said, a century and a half later, the world still grapples with human trafficking. This is where President Lincoln's Cottage has become a leading light in the museum world for the intersection of mission and action. In 2013, in conjunction with the 150th anniversary of the Emancipation Proclamation, the team at Lincoln's Cottage, in alignment with their philosophy of being a museum of ideas rather than a museum of things, wanted to create a program for students that, in the words of Callie Hawkins, director of programming, "engaged them more deeply than a one off field trip."

"Many folks suggested doing some sort of a leadership program," she said, "but Lincoln and leadership has been done to death. We really wanted to explore how can we give students the tools to BE leaders, rather than just learn ABOUT leadership."

What they came up with is one of the most powerful and impactful museum education programs in the country. "Students Opposing Slavery (SOS) is an award-winning youth education program for students dedicated to continuing Lincoln's fight for freedom by raising awareness about modern slavery within a high-risk population—teenagers."[12] When they say award winning, they mean it. In May of 2016, Students Opposing Slavery received the American Alliance of Museums EdCom Award for Excellence in Programming. In October of 2016 the program was awarded the Presidential Award for Extraordinary Efforts to Combat Trafficking in Persons by Secretary of State John Kerry.

The program itself is a multiday summit that brings young abolitionists from across the country and around the world together to tackle the problem of human trafficking. Currently there are more than one hundred youthful leaders who have gone through the program and now form an international network that strives to fulfill the Lincolnian vision that "all persons held as slaves . . . shall be then, thenceforward, and forever free."[13] Students who participate in the program are able to do so at no cost to themselves. Funding covers travel, lodging, and program participation. In addition to the program itself being a powerful example of civic action, the way the program came to be is a beautiful example of how museums can serve as levers of change in their community.

According to Hawkins, the team at Lincoln's Cottage reached out to organizations working in human trafficking as part of the exhibit that was created
for the 150th anniversary of the Emancipation. "We worked with Polaris,
whose name invokes the North Star and a connection to the history of the Underground Railroad, to develop content for the exhibit, and it was a successful
exhibit. Colleges and universities were sending students to learn about human
trafficking—in part because there was no other place to go to learn about it."

After the exhibit, the CEO and founder of the Polaris Project visited President Lincoln's Cottage with four local high school students who wanted to
do something to address the problem of human trafficking, which Polaris
describes as "a $150 billion industry that robs 25 million around the world of
their freedom."[14] The students wanted to start a program, and they wanted it
to live on beyond a single summit. Six years later, Polaris, and alumni return
to continue the work. Here, President Lincoln's Cottage is performing another
civic action, bringing members of the community (students, nonprofits, and
the museum) together to work on serious issues.

"It was important to us that the work be team driven," said Hawkins, "so
we collaborated on the rules on engagement. The students did not want to
hear from adults three times a week about what they should do." Instead,
they wanted to be a part of creating that solution. The museum provided that
opportunity. Student agency remains a keystone of SOS, and the opening

Figure 5.2.   Students gather in front of Lincoln's Cottage in Washington, DC
Photo courtesy of the Ronald Reagan Presidential Foundation and Institute

session for the summit is always led by a program alumnus. What results is the next generation of abolitionists empowered by the legacy of the Great Emancipator, and a through-line that extends from the specific history and mission of the institution, to the action and benefit produced in the real world.

If your visitors care enough about an issue to look at its historic context and come to have a deeper understanding of both the causes and impact of issues in the community, they might be inclined to feel like someone should do something about that issue.

Table 5.4. Museum Profile: President Lincoln's Cottage

Location	Washington, DC
Type of Museum	Historic Home, Presidential Site
Annual Visitors	~30,000 (2019)
Staff	11 full-time 9 part-time
Budget	$1.4 million (2018)
Collection	Several permanent exhibits; President Lincoln's Cottage at the Soldiers' Home

VOLUNTEERING AND PUBLIC SERVICE

Earlier in this chapter we explored the ways in which museums could serve as polling stations, creating an opportunity for the members of their community to conduct one of the most basic units of civic action: casting a vote. What is a little trickier is what happens at the other end of that vote. Museums are prohibited by their nonprofit status from participating in political campaigns, either directly or indirectly, or for or against a candidate. This goes for every office from the presidency down to the local level. At risk of losing their nonprofit status, museums cannot have candidates make campaign speeches at their institutions, use funds to advocate for or against a candidate, donate money to a campaign, link to or support a candidate on the website, or even invite multiple candidates to speak at an event where the questions might suggest that an organization favors one candidate over another. Museums CAN engage in nonpartisan activities including voter registration drives regardless of political party, hosting candidate debates for local or national office, or conduct voter education so long as the activities fulfill the organizational mission.

How then can a museum encourage public service and support those in their community who aspire to serving in government? Connecticut's Old State House offers a way.

Connecticut has a long, proud history of constitutional government. Since 1959[15] Connecticut has been nicknamed the Constitution State. Today, every license plate in the state bears this nickname, not because of the famous Connecticut Compromise that was essential to the drafting of the US Constitution, but because some historians argue that Connecticut has the oldest written constitution in the world, dating back to 1639. Former Connecticut chief justice Simeon Baldwin wrote in 1925, "Connecticut . . . made for herself the first real Constitution, in the modern sense, known to mankind."

Like President Lincoln's Cottage, whose work in civic engagement ties powerfully to their history and mission, Connecticut's Old State House, built in 1796 as the seat of government in Connecticut, ties the unique history of their physical space to a broader mission centered on inclusive democracy. Visitors to their website are greeted with the following:

> Welcome to the home of 360-degree democracy. What does that mean? Simple: the past shapes the future. Government represents the governed. Leaders—of every kind—were once just regular people like you and me. Here at Connecticut's Old State House—the very spot where Connecticut's democracy was born—you'll learn about how it was born and who made it happen.
>
> You'll meet people who went from ordinary to history-making by standing up for what they believed: and maybe think about where you fit in to "government by the people" yourself. [16]

The museum itself is a national landmark and historic site, and it operates, says Sally Whipple, executive director, "at the intersection of history and civics." There are six full-time staff members, and their collective focus is on civic work.

"We're set up a bit differently than many nonprofits," says Whipple. "About twenty years ago, the organization started as a public affairs network. CPAN (Connecticut Public Affairs Network) is basically CSPAN for the State of Connecticut." The Old State House was previously run by the Connecticut Historical Society, but it did not work financially, so the city put out a call for proposals to take over operations of the facility. CPAN won the bid. CPAN's initiatives "are designed to inform and engage audiences of all ages, to give them the information and skills to be effective modern citizens."[17] So together they work on the concept of 360-degree democracy. In order to be an effective citizen, folks should be informed and engaged. On the informed front, their programs include Connecticut History Day, the state affiliate of National History Day, which teaches thousands of students across Connecticut how to research and present historical information. They also host students and visitors at the Old State House. "You can't understand the world without history," says Whipple.

On the engaged front, they host a farmers' market designed to bring the community together downtown and a program called Kid Governor. To help students better understand how state government works, they launched a program where students are able to run for the office of governor. In 2015, the Connecticut legislature passed new social science frameworks for students across the state based on the "C3 Framework" discussed earlier in the chapter. So many teachers, history organizations, and museums began to think very seriously about history beyond the memorization of facts and figures.

"How do we inspire action?" asked Brian Cofrancesco, head of Kid Governor at the Connecticut Democracy Center (an initiative of CPAN). So, they took the example of student mock legislatures and applied that model to the state level. The program is focused on access, so it is offered free of charge to all schools, teachers, and students. They created a series of lessons designed for teachers to be able to implement without being experts on the ins and outs of state government because in the fifth grade, where the program is offered, the teachers are elementary school generalists, charged with teaching their students across all subjects.

"Students who run for Kid Governor," said Cofrancesco, "work to identify a community issue they want to see changed. They then have to put together a platform focused on a single issue and share a three-point plan of action for how they plan to work on that issue." That platform then becomes the basis of their campaign for Kid Governor. In the past, students have focused on a wide range of topics, including bullying, diversity, helping the elderly, foster care, and animal abuse. Each participating school can nominate one candidate for Kid Governor. The candidate then produces a video explaining why they should be elected Kid Governor. Several outside experts, including a former Kid Governor, review the submissions and select a diverse group of students and issues as seven finalists. Thousands of participating fifth grade students from across the state then review the platforms of the candidates and cast their votes. You might be surprised to know that not a single campaign video is a vicious attack ad. It's amazing. The students are often better at a civil democracy than the folks who run to represent them.

Connecticut's most recent Kid Governor met Connecticut's governor along with all six executive branch officers and Representative Jahana Hayes, former National Teacher of the Year, and Connecticut's first African American female representative in Congress. The Kid Governor is linked to the history of governance in the state because the historic governor's office in the Old State House also serves as the office for the Kid Governor. There is also an exhibit on the experience of the Kid Governor as part of the interpretation of the Old State House.

The program is so successful that the model has been adopted by the secretary of state's office in Oregon and the New Hampshire Institute for Civics Education. The team is working with both the National Governors Association and the National Association of Secretaries of State to expand the program across the country. So, it is possible to support candidates for office, inspire a love for history, and build community without impacting nonprofit status.

Table 5.5. Museum Profile: Connecticut's Old State House

Location	Hartford, CT
Type of Museum	Historic Site, National Landmark
Annual Visitors	10–12,000 visitors annually to site 30,000 participate in Farmers' Market 6,500 participate in Kid Governor program 6,000 participate in Connecticut History Day
Staff	6 full-time
Budget	It's complicated
Collection	Old State House; dozens of artifacts from "Connecticut's amazing and eccentric history"

OTHER FORMS OF CIVIC ACTION AND ENGAGEMENT

Once someone is inclined to "do something" about an issue or a group of issues, there really is no limit to the ways in which museums can promote and foster both civic action and civic engagement. As we've explored in this chapter and throughout the book, the best sort of impact a museum can have in its community lies at the intersection of mission and the needs of the community, region, country, and world. The examples above are just the very tip of the iceberg, as many museums across the country do remarkable work at the intersection of mission and need. Ultimately, what your museum can do in this space is a combination of mission, budget, bandwidth, and imagination.

At the Skirball Cultural Center in Los Angeles, elementary school students participate in the Build a Better World Program. They explore an interactive exhibit that tells the story of Noah's Ark, become familiar with the flood narrative, and when they emerge, like Noah, they see an opportunity to "build a better world." The Skirball leverages their position as a community convener to bring together the exhibit, local nonprofits, and students to take civic action. Elementary school students have, as a result of this program, worked with local nonprofits to provide resources to the homeless, started on-campus recycling programs, created play spaces for shelter animals, planted seeds to promote healthy ecosystems, and more.[18]

At Morven Park, a historic home in Leesburg, Virginia, the education team takes the concept of civic engagement out into the community schools. They work with students at their school to identify issues in the community that need to be fixed and empower the students with the tools to fix them. They advocate for four civic ideas that are central to the core of their work: Your Voice Matters, Examine Issues, Take Responsibility, and Make an Impact. One success story from their work involves working with local high school students on a parking problem. Students were frustrated that it took up to forty-five minutes after school to exit the parking lot. School administrators had acknowledged the problem more than fifteen years earlier, but had never found a solution. The students worked to identify a better flow of traffic, made signs, and within a year had cut the time to exit the lot to less than half. Though many of the students who participate in these offsite programs might not actually visit the historic home, they would certainly argue, based on the more than two hours of parking lot time they've been given back each week, that the museum helped produce a benefit for them.

The New-York Historical Society and the Smithsonian National Museum of American History have programs designed to support green card holders preparing to take the naturalization test. They leverage their collections and resources to help prepare these future citizens, and they have helped thousands of people to become American citizens. The historical society hosts the naturalization ceremonies that represent the culmination of this process. So impactful is the program that Justice Ruth Bader Ginsburg offered to lead such a ceremony. According to a 2018 article in the *New York Times*:

> Justice Ginsburg told them that her own father arrived in this country at 13 with no fortune and no ability to speak English, and yet, she would soon be administering the oath of citizenship to them as a member of the highest court in the land.
>
> Justice Ginsburg had read about the program in the *Times*. "I thought it was a grand idea," Justice Ginsburg said. "So, I wrote to N.Y.H.S. and said if ever I am in town when they had a naturalization ceremony, I would be glad to participate."[19]

A traveling exhibit, called Washed Ashore, which takes plastic that has been pulled from the sea and turns it into sculptures of sea life in an effort to raise awareness of the impact of plastic on the world's oceans, has appeared at more than thirty zoos, aquariums, and other museums and public spaces, raising awareness and causing visitors to change their habits when it comes to the use of plastics.

CONCLUSION

Civic action and sustained civic engagement should be the ultimate goals of any museum that takes seriously its civic mission. Action, in and of itself, should not the goal. Rather, an effective integration of knowledge, mindset, and skillset should produce informed action and sustained civic engagement over time. Museums do best to support this when they focus on the intersection of their institutional mission and the needs of the community.

NOTES

1. "Potential Energy." Wikipedia. Accessed December 27, 2019. https://en.wikipedia.org/wiki/Potential_energy.

2. Anheier, Helmut K., and Stefan Toepler, eds. 2010. *International Encyclopedia of Civil Society*. New York: Springer.

3. Ehrlich, Thomas, ed. 2000. *Civic Responsibility and Higher Education*. Westport, CT: Oryx Press.

4. "The College, Career, and Civic Life: C3 Framework for Social Studies State Standards: Guidance for Enhancing the Rigor of K–12 Civics, Economics, Geography, and History." 2013. Silver Spring, MD: National Council for the Social Studies (NCSS).

5. NCSS. 2013. "C3 Framework."

6. "Civic Life in America: Key Findings on the Civic Health of the Nation." 2010. Washington, DC: Corporation for National and Community Service and the National Conference on Citizenship.

7. Hyde, Charles A. 2018. "Why Museums Should Be Proud Polling Sites." *Smithsonian*, October 29, 2018. https://www.smithsonianmag.com/history/why-museums-should-be-proud-polling-sites-180970647/.

8. Hyde. 2018. "Why Museums Should Be Proud Polling Sites."

9. "U.S. Census Bureau QuickFacts: Simi Valley City, California." Accessed January 3, 2020. https://www.census.gov/quickfacts/simivalleycitycalifornia.

10. "U.S. Census Bureau QuickFacts: Sweetwater City, Texas." Accessed January 3, 2020. https://www.census.gov/quickfacts/sweetwatercitytexas.

11. Mast, Erin Carlson. 2018. "Proving the Power of Place: President Lincoln′s Cottage Visitor Impact Study." National Trust for Historic Preservation: Preservation Leadership Forum, May 7, 2018. https://forum.savingplaces.org/blogs/special-contributor/2018/05/07/proving-the-power-of-place-president-lincolns-cott.

12. "Students Opposing Slavery: We are the Generation that Says Enough." 2020. President Lincoln's Cottage. Accessed June 6, 2020. https://www.lincolncottage.org/education/sos/.

13. Emancipation Proclamation, January 1, 1863; Presidential Proclamations, 1791–1991; Record Group 11; General Records of the United States Government; National Archives. https://www.archives.gov/historical-docs/emancipation-proclamation.

14. "Polaris." 2020. Polaris. Accessed January 6, 2020. https://polarisproject.org/.

15. National Constitution Center (NCC) Staff. 2014. "The Debate over Connecticut as the Constitution State." Yahoo! News, January 14, 2014. https://news.yahoo.com/debate-over-connecticut-constitution-state-110213247.html.

16. "Visit Connecticut's 1796 State House." 2020. Connecticut's Old State House. Accessed January 2, 2020. https://www.cga.ct.gov/osh/default.asp.

17. "Connecticut Public Affairs Network (CPAN)." 2018. Connecticut Public Affairs Network (CPAN), January 15, 2018. https://ctpublicaffairsnetwork.org/programs.

18. "Building a Better World." 2020. Skirball Cultural Center, January 21, 2020. https://www.skirball.org/education/building-better-world.

19. Robbins, Liz. 2018. "Justice Ginsburg Urges New Citizens to Make America Better." *New York Times*, April 10, 2018. https://www.nytimes.com/2018/04/10/nyregion/supreme-court-ruth-bader-ginsburg-naturalization-ceremony.html.

6

Toolkit for Democracy

What's important is that you have a faith in people, that they're basically good and smart, and if you give them tools, they'll do wonderful things with them. It's not the tools that you have faith in—tools are just tools. They work, or they don't work. It's people you have faith in or not.

—Steve Jobs

Discover the tools to build your own vision.

—Mary Anne Radmacher

In the opening chapter I shared the famous story of Benjamin Franklin's response/warning when he emerged from the convening that produced the Constitution of the United States.

"A republic . . . if you can keep it."

Over the course of the past several chapters, we have explored some of the ways in which museums have done their part, in their communities, to keep it:

They collect, share, and create civic knowledge.
They teach and cultivate civic mindset.
They empower their communities with the civic skills necessary for a more
  perfect union.
They take and inspire civic action.

Though it might be nice, after all this work, after all this thinking, designing, engaging with internal and external stakeholders, creation, adaptation, public unveilings, community partnerships, storytelling, training, the opening and closing of exhibits, events, public programs . . . though it would be nice to sit back, relax, and enjoy a quiet moment of achievement, to sit by the fire with a nice cup of tea or wine, and bask in the warmth of the success of something good—the truth is that the civic work of museums is never done. Just as history evolves as it is reinterpreted through modern lenses, new histories, expanded voices, and additional evidence; as art is preserved or presented in a different context; as science evolves with new discoveries and more powerful technology; and as beautiful, cutting-edge new buildings eventually become dated and in need of repair, new pipes, and a fresh coat of paint—so, too, evolves the civic mission of museums.

In some ways the work of museum professionals is similar to the work of gardeners.

My grandfather, Richard Ransom Wilson, was both the first gardener I ever met and the reason civic learning has long been a passion of mine. A former US Marine, he was briefly deployed to Japan in the wake of the atomic bomb before serving in the Korean War. My first civics lesson came at a college football game. USC, his alma mater, was playing Notre Dame at the LA Coliseum. I couldn't have been more than eight years old. I vividly remember getting a hot dog at the concession stand, and then scooching our way through the massive crowd to our seats. I was hungry, and really looking forward to eating. The sounds of the crowd, the colors, the yelling, the blue sky, the cold air of late fall—it was a bit overwhelming. I sat in the hard plastic seat, soaking it all in. All of a sudden, my grandfather stood up quickly from his seat.

I took a bite of my hot dog.

He looked at me expectantly.

I started to take another bite of my hot dog.

Then, with his massive hands, my grandfather, one of the strongest men I ever knew, picked me up by my shirt collar until I was standing—not rough, mind you—strong, firm, and smooth.

My grandfather was a man of few words. He jutted his chin toward the armed forces color guard that had marched onto the field and now stood at the base of the goalpost in anticipation of the national anthem.

"When you see the flag," he whispered, "you should stand."

That was my first civics lesson. It took years for me to understand that his words meant more than "you should stand." That behind his words were his own experiences as a soldier, memories of friends who died in battle, an appreciation of the long and complicated history of freedom in the United States, and a lived understanding of just how hard it can be to "keep it" in a republic like ours.

He exemplified the notion of hard work—owning and operating a gas station near the University of Southern California to help pay for college, he worked for a car dealership, and eventually worked as a regional manager for Sears. He would leave my grandmother, my mom, and my aunt and uncle on Monday, drive around, visit the Sears stores in the Northeast, and then return home to Pennsylvania on Thursday or Friday. He did this for years. In his early fifties, the increasingly devastating effects of macular degeneration, which my grandmother linked to radiation exposure during the war, meant early retirement and a move to Southern California. Never one to relax or take it easy, my grandfather dedicated much of the next thirty-plus years of his life to tending his garden.

They had a massive backyard, and every day was the same. He'd wake up early, eat his breakfast, go on a walk, and then spend the morning in the garden. A row of citrus trees lined the left side of the yard, and when the lemons were ripe, my brother and I would make lemonade with my grandmother and sell it at the side of the road. In the back were a variety of trees, bird feeders, wooden planters filled with strawberries, tomatoes, and other fruits and vegetables. The right side of the yard was covered in ice plants, and rows of clay pots filled with various plants, fruits, and vegetables, whatever seeds might be in season down at the store. He'd start along the right side of the house, and over the course of the day he'd make his way slowly around, adjusting pots, pulling weeds, his fingernails dark from the soil. His hands were soft, worn, and smelled of earth. In his later years, as his sight faded completely, he'd navigate the yard by intuition and feel. Sometimes he'd only make it halfway around the yard. He'd grab a footstool or lean a ladder for the branches he couldn't reach. One day, when he was well into his eighties, my grandmother went out to play bridge with some friends. He lost his balance and fell from the ladder. He was on the ground in pain for hours, unable, with limited balance and sight, to stand. It wasn't long until they sold the house and moved to a facility without a garden.

As they were moving, the family came together to help downsize. The entire wall of the left side of the garage was filled with my grandfather's gardening tools. The hand tools—shovels, clippers, trowels, the cultivating claws, and mismatched gloves with holes worn through the fingers, were hung, in various states of rust and decay, on the pegboard with a neat precision. Leaned against the corner of a cabinet were the larger tools—hoes, rakes, gardening shears. We held a garage sale, and we laid the tools out together, and they took up nearly one-quarter of the driveway. Apparently, it takes a lot of tools to tend a garden.

In *Gardens of Democracy*, Eric Liu and Nick Hanauer explain why gardens are such a powerful metaphor for the work of democracy:

> Effective gardening requires the right setting: fertile soil, good light, water.
>
> It requires a strong view as to what should and should not be grown.
>
> It requires a loving willingness to tend constantly, to fertilize and nurture what we seed.
>
> It requires a hard-headed willingness to weed what does not belong.
>
> Great gardeners would never simply "let nature take its course." They take responsibility for their gardens.
>
> Great gardeners assume change in weather and circumstance. They adapt.
>
> Great gardens are sustainable only with continuous investment and renewal. Great gardeners turn the soil and rotate the plantings.
>
> Human beings, it is said, originated in a garden. Perhaps this is why all of us understand so intuitively what it takes to be great gardeners.[1]

This comparison should resonate powerfully with our colleagues in the botanical gardens, no strangers to maintaining the earth and its bounty, but the metaphor holds true whether your institution is centered on history, art, science, culture, children, nature, zoos and aquariums, libraries, archives or any of the other ways we subcategorize our museums. So in this chapter, we'll be exploring some of the many tools you might find helpful as you tend your civic garden, and use some of the words of Liu and Hanauer to select our tools.

In doing so, this section is not meant as a didactic prescription. I am not suggesting that all museums must use these specific tools in a very specific and prescribed way. To quote Stephen Weil, "The public benefit and impact that a museum can provide will never be the same in any two institutions. The real guts and glory of every museum is in its particularity, not in what it does in common with others. As museums vary enormously by discipline, collections, scale, facilities, context, location, funding, and history, so, too, must the mix of benefits that can provide be varied from institution to institution. What we can generalize about, though, are some of the elements that might be included in that mix—some of the different ways in which museums might contribute to the better lives of those who use them."[2] So what follows is a general toolkit meant to explore, broadly speaking, some of the ways your museum might approach this work.

CIVIC MISSION TOOLKIT TIP #1: ENSURE THE RIGHT SETTING

"Fertile soil, good light, water." Or, to put it in "museum speak"—the intersection of mission, the needs of the community, and the ability and bandwidth of staff to execute programs, develop exhibits, and integrate with the community. In a garden, if you have the right soil but not enough light and water, the plants may grow, but they won't thrive. If you have plenty of water and light but no soil, nothing is going to grow. The same is true in museum work. Perhaps an exhibit or a program aligns well with your mission but doesn't fulfill any specific community need. Visitors and community members might see the exhibit, or participate in the program, but that doesn't necessarily mean that your museum has produced the public benefit that is core to the civic mission of museums. Likewise, if you have a program that is mission aligned, and fits well with the needs of the community, but your staff is committed to fifteen other projects as you strive to be everything for everyone, the ability to deliver that program in meaningful, lasting, and impactful ways is extremely limited. Like the plant in the garden, it might grow, but it won't thrive.

I remember walking into the curatorial offices at our museum a month or so ahead of a new exhibit. The curator had drawn a triangle on the board. The three corners had been labeled FAST, CHEAP, and GOOD. Beside the triangle he had written in big block letters, "PICK TWO." I chuckled as I imagined the frustrating conversations that must have led to this diagram.

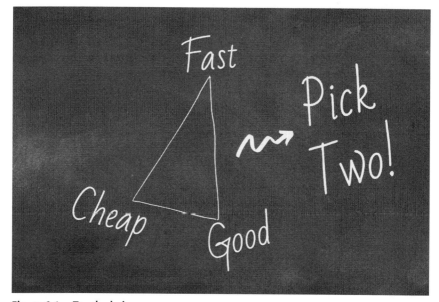

Figure 6.1. Tough choices
Created by author

Whereas a new exhibit might only be able to deliver on two of the three requirements above, it is absolutely necessary for a museum to have the soil, light, and water in proper proportion to deliver on its civic mission.

In the previous chapter, we explored how Lincoln's Cottage Students Opposed to Slavery program was a prime example of "Fertile Soil, Good Light, and Water."

Fertile Soil: Organizational Mission

- Mission: "Reveal the true Lincoln and continue the fight for freedom."
- Vision: "Plant the seeds of Lincoln's brave ideas around the world so that all people, everywhere, can be free."[3]

Good Light: Needs of the Community

- Human trafficking remains a worldwide problem, with more than twenty-five million victims.

Water: Ability of Staff and Community to Take Action

- The combination of Lincoln's Cottage staff, students, and nonprofit collaborators come together to cultivate young freedom fighters worldwide.

The EdCom Awards for museum education programs are ripe with examples of programs, innovations, and people who exemplify work that exists in the nexus of Fertile Soil, Good Light, and Water. In 2019, EdCom gave the Award for Innovation in Museum Education to the Vizcaya Museum and Gardens for their Urban Farming School Program. Vizcaya is located in Miami, a city, that like many southeastern US coastal towns that seem to be under annual threat of hurricanes. Vizcaya itself was damaged by Hurricane Irma in 2017 and prepared extensively for Hurricane Dorian in 2019 as well. It exists in the sometimes dangerous, sometimes beautiful, confluence of man and nature. Environmental sustainability is a matter of survival for Vizcaya. Its education program, the Vizcaya Urban Farming School Program, works with local public schools to educate students on the importance of "current agricultural practices, environmental stewardship and nutritional health."[4]

Fertile Soil: Organizational Mission

- Mission: "Preserving Vizcaya's cultural and environmental resources to engage people in connecting with the past, understanding the present and shaping the future."

- Vision: "Vizcaya is an enduring, inclusive and innovative place that inspires people to embrace the cultural vitality and environmental sustainability of the world around us."[5]

Good Light: Needs of the Community

- "Journey mapping demonstrates the carbon footprint and environmental impact of transporting foods to our community. These lessons develop knowledge about harvesting and using fruits and vegetables for nutritional health, and demonstrate how we can reduce carbon footprints by growing locally."[6]

Water: Ability of Staff and Community to Take Action

- The team at Vizcaya works hand in hand with the Miami-Dade County Public School system in supporting existing curriculum and informing teachers and students on ways to reduce carbon footprints, essential to the long-term survival of both Vizcaya and the community.

So regardless of your institution's mission, community, and human ability to take action, be sure to take a deep breath, assess all three, and ensure that you have plenty of each before moving forward.

Figure 6.2. In order to successfully deliver on your organization's civic mission, you must ensure you have the right mix of soil, light, and water
Created by author

CIVIC MISSION TOOLKIT TIP #2:
WHAT SHOULD AND SHOULD NOT BE GROWN

In the introduction of *Fostering Empathy Through Museums*, Elif Gokcigdem writes, "Museums hold a mirror to our collective behavior, knowledge, conscience, complex histories, and values. Through their educational mission, they can provide safe and critical context to fostering empathy through experiential learning, storytelling, artistic expression, dialogue, and contemplation."[7] Just as Gokcigdem lists the many ways museums can foster empathy, there are also a seemingly infinite array of options for how we leverage our collections, our team, and our community to best produce a civic impact. Empathy, writes Gokcigdem, is "our inherent ability to perceive and share the feelings of another. . . . Not only are we wired to connect, but also to find ways to serve the greater good." In this way, empathy is a key component of the civic mission of museums. We must both forge civic connections and serve the greater good. In the course of doing this work, we must make choices about HOW best to do this work. Just as a gardener must make choices about what should and should not be grown, museums must choose how best to make an impact. Two phrases that can be common in museums:

We can't be everything to everybody.
That's a great idea. Who is going to do it?

Because we can't do everything, because we don't have the capacity or ability to run with every bright idea or opportunity for collaboration, we must make smart choices about what to do, and who to do it with. What program will make the greatest impact? Which investment of time yields the greatest civic "return on investment? These are questions that must be asked both before embarking on a project, and again in the process of evaluation. When we seek to collect, curate, share, and cocreate civic knowledge, our options for how best to do that are limited only by our imaginations. Making the right choices is key. Recall the lunch counter from Greensboro. In one museum, it makes sense to "grow" an interactive interpretation that engages the audience. In another, it makes sense to "grow" an opportunity to take a seat at the counter. At another, the story is told through the lens of its place in the evolution of the city. Visitors build empathy through role-playing, experiencing the intense emotions and anger, and through narrative interpretation. That empathy allows them to connect to both history and the lessons of history that can be applied in the present.

Similarly, we examined museums whose staff made choices about what to "grow" as they created programs that developed civic mindsets, civic skillsets, and civic action.

Choosing is hard, especially in the nonprofit world, and especially for the many selfless museum professionals who choose to work in museums because the believe in the power of art, history, science, play, culture, or whatever their subject matter is, to make the world a better place. If we could just forge one more community partnership with this very deserving group, we could increase our impact! We could make the world a better place. And, as professionals, we know that our institutions have power—to bring people together, to tell stories, to have a positive impact. Often, we want to say yes to everything. Greg McKeown could be writing about museum professionals when he says, "They accept every opportunity presented. They throw themselves into every assignment. They tackle every challenge with gusto. They try to do it all."[8]

He goes on to explain why making a choice is difficult, "By definition they involve saying no to something or several somethings, and that can feel like a loss." This is especially true for those who work in a profession focused on helping others and building community. A teacher might have trouble saying no to a student who asks for an answer to a difficult question, even if struggling to answer the question might benefit the student in the long run. A museum education manager might have trouble saying no to a local after-school group that requests permission to use the museum for a meeting after hours, even if those extra hours and setup mean negatively impacting preparation for another program or initiative, or having to put off, again, taking the time to evaluate a program, or do some long-term planning. McKeown argues that when we say yes to everything, "When we forget our ability to choose, we learn to be helpless. Drip by drip we allow our power to be taken away until we end up becoming a function of other people's choices—or even a function of our own past choices. In turn, we surrender our power to choose."

In choosing what programs to do, in being intentional about how we can best and most efficiently administer our limited time, resources, and talent, we embrace the power that comes as a result of working with our institution and the community. Making choices, saying no to the programs that exist because "we've always done them," is choosing individual and institutional power. And choosing to embrace civic power means we must also choose to embrace the attendant civic responsibility.

CIVIC MISSION TOOLKIT TIP #3: TAKE RESPONSIBILITY

Eleanor Roosevelt said, "In the long run, we shape our lives, and we shape ourselves. The process never ends until we die. And the choices we make are ultimately our own responsibility." Once you, your team, your department, your institution, and/or your community makes the choice about what to grow, you must take the responsibility to ensure it continues to have the fertile soil, good light, and water it needs to thrive. For example, immigration is key to the history of New York. One of the most recognizable landmarks in the world, the Statue of Liberty, is often seen as a beacon to immigrants. Inside the statue is a bronze plaque cast with the text of Emma Lazarus's famous poem, "The New Colossus," which includes the legendary lines:

Give me your tired, your poor,
Your huddled masses yearning to breathe free,
The wretched refuse of your teeming shore.
Send these, the homeless, tempest-tost to me,
I lift my lamp beside the golden door!

Figure 6.3. The Statue of Liberty
Photo by Ronie

The story of New York is rooted in the story of immigration, in the story of the hope of successive waves of the "tempest-tost," generation after generation, coming to the United States. This idea that the United States served as a beacon for immigrants dates back to the 1630 sermon of John Winthrop who told fellow Puritans before the early settlement of Boston that "their new community would be 'as a city upon a hill.'"[9] His sermon was largely forgotten for hundreds of years but became a powerful and lasting symbol for the promise of America in the last half of the twentieth century. John F. Kennedy referenced the "city on the hill" prior to his inauguration and reminded his audience that, "For of those to whom much is given, much is required."[10] Ronald Reagan, in his farewell address to the nation, spoke of "the shining city" on the hill and described it as "a tall, proud city built on rocks stronger than oceans, wind-swept, God-blessed, and teeming with people of all kinds living in harmony and peace; a city with free ports that hummed with commerce and creativity. And if there had to be city walls, the walls had doors and the doors were open to anyone with the will and the heart to get here."[11] Other politicians, including Barack Obama, Mitt Romney, and others have used the same imagery, that the United States, since its earliest days, has served as a beacon of freedom throughout the world. Though the imagery of the city on the hill is uplifting, the poem inspiring, and the statue an impressive and welcoming site in the harbor, the reality of the American immigration story is much more complex.

The Brooklyn Historical Society (BHS), which recently announced a merger with the Brooklyn Public Library to become the Center for Brooklyn History, has taken responsibility for collecting and sharing the complex story of the "flood after flood of immigrant populations that have changed Brooklyn over time," says Deborah Schwartz, president and CEO. Since 1863, the BHS has made, "the vibrant history of Brooklyn tangible, meaningful and relevant today."[12] The founders of BHS focused, as you can probably imagine, on the stories of the British and Dutch immigrants who made their way to Brooklyn. Now, BHS is "working hard to make sure Haitian, Muslim, Puerto Rican, and African American communities" have their stories told as well. In an era of simple, black and white, absolutist narratives that can be quickly conveyed on Twitter, in a sound bite, or in a text message, they do the hard but necessary work of telling a complex story in a complex way.

Since 2017, BHS has been working on "a multi-year, public arts and history project to amplify stories of Brooklyn's diverse Muslim communities" called Muslims in Brooklyn. It is built on three key ideas:

1. Muslims in Brooklyn have a long history. Muslim communities have been a part of American life since before the nation's founding; and established Muslim communities have been in Brooklyn for over a century.
2. Muslims in Brooklyn are a diverse people. The lives and work of Muslims in Brooklyn span many ethnicities, cultures, and nationalities.
3. Muslims in Brooklyn are Brooklynites. Muslims have both shaped and been shaped by life in Brooklyn.[13]

For an organization that has taken responsibility for doing the hard work of telling the complex local and national story of immigration, it makes all sorts of powerful connections. The subject matter of the project connects to the history of the local, the history of the nation, and the history of immigration.

Schwartz says that BHS treats "Brooklyn as a microcosm of American history. The local [as a concept] is compelling to people. It is a touchstone for helping the people of Brooklyn understand and respond to the larger American story." She describes their approach as a bit edgy. "We don't think of ourselves as a neutral place. The notion that museums are, or should be, neutral, is not true. We as professionals have a point of view. We embrace a transparency about that. We embrace the idea that history is messy, because there is a reason historians are never done with their work. Even the greatest historians must be reexamined in the light of present day." This is why, even though they are rooted in the history of Brooklyn, much of their public programming explores contemporary issues. Says Schwartz, "Some of the same issues we're facing in the present day are the same things that have happened over and over again throughout history." So taking the responsibility for making the connections between the past and the present is a key part of what makes the BHS work.

In Lois Lowry's Newbery Award–winning *The Giver*, she writes of a dystopic society that has collected all its memories and placed them in the care of a single person. The society has ritual, but no shared memory, no common history. The world is without pain, without death, without war, but also without color and without love. It is a society that has forgotten.

In his farewell address to the nation, President Ronald Reagan said, "If we forget what we did, we won't know who we are. I'm warning of an eradication of the American memory that could result, ultimately, in an erosion of the American spirit."[14] Over the course of the past two decades, instructional time dedicated to history and social studies has declined in schools as more and more time has been devoted to language arts and math instruction. The accountability measures of No Child Left Behind, from 2001, emphasized testing in language arts and math; students are exposed less and less frequently to their community, local, national, and world history. We are, as a nation, forgetting. And, if you recall the statistics of the opening of the book—faith in our political institutions is plummeting and our rating as a leading democracy is falling—is it any wonder? Therefore, museums must take responsibility.

So when your institution decides to take responsibility, follow the example of BHS, and do so in beautiful, complex, and rich ways that serve to empower and uplift the community you serve. Our republic depends on it.

CIVIC MISSION TOOLKIT TIP #4: INVEST AND RENEW

Great gardens are sustainable only with continuous investment and renewal. Great gardeners turn the soil and rotate the plantings.

When committed to the civic mission of museums, when working to keep the republic, it is essential that you, your department, your institution, and your community invest and renew. For you, meaningfully invest your time, your efforts, your attention, and in your network. Read about the work being done at other museums. Think about new ways to do meaningful work. Join a book club at your institution with folks from other departments. Join a local or regional network of museum or civic professionals. Join national networks and organizations. If you want to build community, if you want to create a civic space, you, yourself, must be a civic actor. You must have personal connections to your colleagues and your community if you want to walk the walk.

If your department is creating a new program, invest in it. Be sure you have the time, staff, bandwidth, and resources to do it well. In his 2001 business strategy best seller, *Good to Great,* Jim Collins tells the story of Dave Scott, a legendary triathlete who won the Ironman six time. "In training, Scott would ride his bike 75 miles, swim 20,000 meters, and run 17 miles—on average, every single day . . . he believed that a low-fat, high-carbohydrate diet would give him an extra edge. So, Dave Scott—a man who burned at least 5,000 calories a day in training—would literally rinse his cottage cheese to get the extra fat off."[15] Collins uses this example to show the power of discipline in taking an organization from being merely good to great, and the metaphor works well for museum professionals too. Museum professionals are often masters of plate spinning, working on programming, exhibits, community partnerships, visitor engagement, and raising funds. Sometimes all at once. But if you want your civic garden to grow, you have to invest the time to water, to care, and to weed. You must have the discipline to invest your limited time and energy in the work that most effectively produces that public benefit.

For museums, you must invest in your staff. In a 2019 post on their blog, *Leadership Matters,* Anne Ackerson and Joan Baldwin write to museum leaders, "As leaders, isn't it time you protect your investment in staff? They are, particularly if you also pay healthcare and some form of retirement, a huge portion of your annual budget. Assuming they're good at what they do, don't you want them to stay, to not spend idle hours at work trolling job sites, to be happy, to be creative? How can you *not* invest in them? Everybody wants a diverse workforce. It mirrors the communities we live in, and creates a better product."[16] So once staff invests the time in professional development and departments invest the time and energy to do the work with purpose, institutions should invest in their staff. They should support their professional development, encourage them to grow, and then pay them competitive wages so that the connections they forge in the community will be long-term connections between the institution and the community it serves.

When it comes to turning the soil and rotating the plantings, this works two ways. First, you want to be sure that your team and your institution work iteratively. The world is changing rapidly. It has never been easier to access information and grow networks. Beyond taking the time to invest, you must also take the time to renew. Personally, this might mean using your vacation days to actually take a break, meditate, sit by a pool or the ocean and renew your soul. But it also means that your institution can help with the renewal process when it comes to democracy. You see, the framers of our country built in a process of renewal. Every two years, we have the opportunity as a nation to "renew" the House of Representatives. Every four years, we choose to keep or replace our president. Every six years, our senators are up for election. Each time you cast a vote, you are participating in the process of renewal. Museums, though, can't cast a vote, and because our nonprofit status means we cannot actively endorse candidates, support specific pieces of legislation, or host political events, many museums feel that they should stay away completely from politics.

In a 2018 article for *Forbes* titled, "To Renew our Democracy, Get Back to the Core," contributor Brook Manville cites the work of Stanford professor Josiah Ober in describing the

> must-have conceptual elements that distinguished what democracy first meant— and (as he forcefully argues) still means today. It is a *community* (of citizens, with shared values and traditions) that:
>
> - Chooses to govern itself for three purposes: protecting itself, providing collective welfare, and ensuring a society answerable only to itself ("non-tyranny");
> - Pursues these purposes by embracing three core beliefs (civic freedom, civic equality, and civic dignity for all citizens);
> - Expects its citizens to actively participate in public life, making decisions and taking accountability for what they collectively decide.
>
> Any system of democracy will ultimately fail if this handful of conditions are not met and sustained. Thus, Ober insists, renewing any failing—or even just struggling— democracy must start with a blueprint of this essence.[17]

So how can museums support the process of democratic renewal despite their nonprofit status? I put this question out to Museum Junction, AAM's online community of museum professionals. What is the role of museums when it comes to elections? As you can probably imagine, the responses varied pretty widely.

1. **Support Voting:** You don't have to take a political stance or support a candidate or ballot measure to serve as a voting location. As we explored earlier in the book, the Benjamin Harrison Presidential Site serves as a voting location, as do many museums across the country.

It brings you in contact with local volunteers, shares the message that your institution values the civic act of casting a vote, and centers your institution as a place where civic action can take place. If your institution cannot serve as a polling station, perhaps you can work with local organizations to host a voter registration drive. Lenora Costa of the Longue Vue House & Gardens in New Orleans writes, "On more than one occasion we have been a voter registration location for New Orleans. Our founders were interested in voting rights and worked on voter registration from the 1940s–1970s so we use that as historic precedent for the program. It allows us to relate to an election but not get involved in supporting a person or position."

2. **Host Debates and Inform Voters:** As we've seen earlier in this book, there are many museums that serve as host sites for candidate debates at all levels. The National Constitution Center famously served as a host site for the 2008 Democratic Primary Debate between senators Hillary Clinton and Barack Obama. We explored how the University of New Hampshire hosted a Democratic Primary Debate in 2016, and the Ronald Reagan Presidential Library hosted a Republican Primary Debate in 2015 as well. However, a museum does not have to host a debate with national implications to help its citizens "actively participate in public life." Vivian Zoe, director of the Slater Memorial Museum in Norwich, Connecticut, said, "We host, in our auditorium, local candidate debates."[18] We also explored museums hosting Town Hall events with local, regional, and national officials. Though your institution might not be able to advocate for or support any of these candidates, providing a public forum where citizens can be informed on the issues and the candidates is key in supporting how we choose to be self-governed. Ruth Haus, president of the Living History Farms in Des Moines, Iowa, notes that her site has served as "an iconic gathering place and host [to] many elected officials . . . town halls, forums, rall[ies] etc. We have hosted Vice Presidents Dan Quayle and recently Joe Biden, First Lady Barbara Bush, Presidents Obama and Trump, our Congressman, the US Secretary of Agriculture (Perdue) and a multitude of federal candidates on the campaign trail including US Secretary of State Clinton. Our former Congressman hosted many a town hall here as well. In addition, media outlets have used our site for Iowa Town Halls on immigration and other issues. Most recently, Harris Faulkner hosted a Fox News town hall." In addition, they will serve as a caucus site in the 2020 presidential primaries, and they "plan an education event beforehand for our members and kids to 'caucus for cookies' to teach them about the caucus process which has a rich tradition in rural Iowa communities."[19] So not only are

Figure 6.4.   Living History Farms in Urbandale, Iowa, circa 2007
Photo by Allen Huffman

they hosting caucuses, they are teaching the next generation of citizens about their importance in the political process. Whether you are hosting candidates, or public forums, or local officials or leaders discussing important issues, your institution has the ability to help the community make informed decisions and take action.

3. **Generate Enthusiasm for Elections:** The Harry S Truman Little White House in Key West, Florida, learned to capitalize on the public interest in elections back in 2000. Robert Wolz, executive director emeritus, writes, "Back in 2000 when Florida became the center of Bush/Gore, I immediately set about finding a Palm Beach voting machine and ballot box. Our guests thought it was great fun to have sample ballots with all sorts of chads. In 2004 and every 4 years since, we created a special exhibit entitled 'Every Four Years' and aggressively collected campaign buttons for all the presidential candidates—pro and con. . . . We also tried to locate all the 3rd party candidates: green party, socialists, communists, vegetarian, Freedom party, etc. (you get the point). Most found it fascinating that so many were running that no one ever heard of."

"We try to include convention badges, anything that is truly weird or unusual." In addition to sharing the campaign buttons with their visitors, they also work to explain the oft-misunderstood electoral college to their visitors.

Prior to the 2016 election, our institution hosted "Pizza and Politics," an informal debate watch party aimed at high school and college students. An hour before the debates began, we offered free pizza, took some polls on which issues and candidates resonated with the students, moderated a discussion on polarizations and the divisive election in conjunction with a local nonprofit, and then debriefed the debate. The Hammer Museum in Los Angeles also hosts debate watch parties and runs a "series called Constitution Happy Hour, in which an expert (usually a UCLA professor) discusses an aspect of the Constitution with attendees over drinks," said Susan Edwards, associate director of Digital Content—a fitting way to explore the Constitution indeed.[20]

4. **Once the Election is Over, Keep Going:** At the Monterey Bay Aquarium in Monterey, California, they "created numerous exhibits encouraging, empowering and enabling visitors to communicate with elected officials on topics from marine protected areas to fishing regulations and climate change."[21] Our institution used letters from the presidential archives that students had written to President Reagan to encourage students to research an issue and write a policy recommendation to an elected official who had the power to make a change. The Chester County Historical Society, which has long served as a polling site, also encourages visitors to take "blank post cards" and "write about an issue that was important and 'mail' it to their member of congress (CCHS did the mailing)," said Ellen Endslow, director of Collections/Curator. Whether your institution is an aquarium, an art museum, or a historic site, make a connection between your collection and civic action, and teach your visitors and community how to make their voices heard in elections and beyond.

BRINGING IT ALL TOGETHER

In a 1988 speech at the annual gathering of the Canadian Museums Association, Stephen Weil said, "To focus museum rhetoric on the socially beneficial aspects of a museum would ultimately be to invite discussion on a wide range of political and moral issues that could well pit trustees against staff members and staff members against one another."[22] Since 1988, our country has grown increasingly far apart on political issues, and the wide range of issues that have become political and pit people against each other is growing. Politics is ever-present in nearly every aspect of life. We draw sides when an NFL player takes

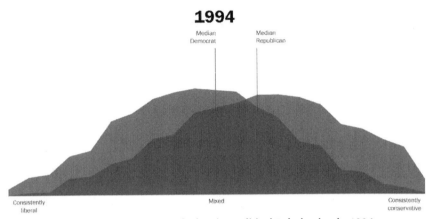

Figure 6.5.   Data from Pew Research showing Political Polarization in 1994
Data from Pew Research

a knee during the national anthem. We draw sides each year when the nominees for the Oscars are announced. We draw sides when decades-old video or audio footage of a public figure comes to light. We exist in the era of cancel culture.

With museums sometimes struggling to make ends meet, with federal and local funding constantly under threat, political power at the local and national level shifting rapidly back and forth, and volatility in the government and financial markets, being the target of the next round of politically charged ire is a dangerous proposition for any museum. At a time when it seems like the very fabric of society and democracy itself is coming unraveled, it feels safer to weather the storm. It feels safer to board up the windows, weatherproof the doors, and cautiously watch, hoping and praying that the storm will pass, because in a garden, there are seasons. There is the season of pouring rain

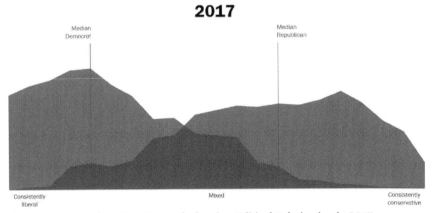

Figure 6.6.   Data from Pew Research showing Political Polarization in 2017
Data from Pew Research

and floods, and in those times we do our best to ensure the soil doesn't get washed away. There is a season of sun and heat, and we work hard to ensure the ground isn't baked into a thick crust of clay, so hard and dry that no plant can survive. In the morning there is dew. At night there is frost. The gardener must be ever vigilant.

Elaine Heumann Gurian writes, "You might think of institutions of memory as savings banks for our souls . . . we regard institutions of memory as important to our collective well-being. Accordingly, we must begin to discuss the preservation of these organizations not because they add to the quality of life . . . but because without them, we come apart."[23] Whether you look at the work of Robert Putnam, whose *Bowling Alone* documents the long, slow, steady decline in the way that communities attend public meetings, volunteer, and join clubs and organizations; or consider the Pew research that shows Americans are increasingly dividing into political tribes and sorting themselves by region; or just follow the hurricane-like storm of dialogue after every public scandal, driven by tempests of righteous outrage on all sides of an issue, only to melt quickly away when the next issue du jour briefly captures the public imagination—by Friday, many of us have forgotten what we were so incensed by on Monday. It seems, at times, like museums have very little power to make an impact, to build community, or to alter the increasingly devastating speed and power that drive public discourse. We are, to paraphrase Gurian, coming apart.

So what do we do? Do we simply accept that our fate is inevitable? Is the speed of our decline too fast? Are the political, media, technological, and societal factors that have, for decades now, driven us increasingly father apart simply too powerful and overwhelming for us to make a difference? If you've read this far, I don't suspect you are the type of person to accept that we are destined to an inevitable and irrevocable decline. I expect that you are the type of person, the type of citizen, and the type of professional who believes we have the ability to determine our fate. In fact, you might look around your museum and see the story of those who came before us, who believed they, too, could make a difference for the better.

In his 1988 speech on the proper business of museums, Stephen Weil asked, "The question we must ultimately ask ourselves is this: do our museums make a real difference in, and do they have a positive impact on, the lives of other people? . . . if so, if the life of the community is richer for the work we do, if we make an important and positive difference in the lives of others, then the zeal we bring to our daily work will have been well rewarded, and our own working lives well spent."[24]

Are we making a difference for the better? Are we, as museum professionals dedicated to the exhausting work of building a community and preserving democracy, living lives well spent?

As part of a recent talk to roughly nine hundred students, ranging from elementary through high school, Medal of Honor recipient and Navy Seal Britt Slabinski talked about the symbolism of the flag of the United States. He shared that many are taught about the various elements of the flag. Many know that the fifty stars represent the fifty states of the union, and that the thirteen stripes signify the thirteen colonies of Great Britain that came together to rise up against the most powerful military in the world, in order to form "a more perfect union." Fewer know about the significance of the colors—that white symbolizes purity and innocence, that blue stands for vigilance and justice, and red stands for the bravery of those who've defended the country and the Constitution. Most know that these elements, the stars and stripes, the red, white, and blue, come together to form the flag. We see it flown over our museums, schools, displayed in offices, auditoriums, on the shoulders of uniforms, or encased on display in our museums. These elements together are instantly recognizable. What almost no one sees, argues Slabinski, and no one really thinks about, "is the thing that holds all of that together—which is, of course, the thread. No one pays any attention to it. But do you ever see a flag blowing in the wind? Sometimes they are just getting shredded at the end and that last little piece of fabric, that last little piece of thread, is just holding on. It's giving all it's got in the storm. It's doing its part until it can't give anymore, and then the next one picks up and holds. The next teammate in the line picks up and holds on for us. This is the way I look at citizenship. All of us have our duty, going unseen, unrecognized, holding the line . . . and if we do our part, we hold the line."[25]

And so we do. Because as museum professionals, we embrace the power afforded to us as individuals. We embrace the responsibility that comes with that power, the responsibility to hold the line as institutions of memory, to tell the stories of those who have tended the civic gardens and ensured that they thrived during the fiercest of storms and the driest of droughts. We know that, as stated by Dr. Martin Luther King Jr., "The arc of the moral universe is long, but it bends toward justice"—and that the story of how our republic endures the dark days of polarization and sorting and the loss of civil discourse is now being written. When that story is done, it, too, will be kept by an institution of memory, and it will say that museums did their part.

NOTES

1. Liu, Eric, and Nick Hanauer. 2011. *Gardens of Democracy: A New American Story of Citizenship, the Economy and the Role of Government*. Seattle: Sasquatch Books.

2. Weil, Stephen E. 2004. *Rethinking the Museum and Other Meditations*. Washington: Smithsonian Books, 50.

3. "About." President Lincoln's Cottage. Accessed January 24, 2020. https://www.lincolncottage.org/about/.

4. "Innovation, Schools and Urban Farming." 2019. Vizcaya. Accessed September 19, 2019. https://vizcaya.org/posts/vizcayas-urban-farming-school-program-recognized-for-innovation-in-museum-education/.

5. "Frequently Asked Questions." 2020. Vizcaya. Accessed January 29, 2020. https://vizcaya.org/about/frequently-asked-questions/.

6. "Innovation, Schools, and Urban Farming." 2019. Vizcaya.

7. Gokcigdem, Elif M. 2016. *Fostering Empathy through Museums*. Blue Ridge Summit: Rowman & Littlefield.

8. McKeown, Greg. 2014. *Essentialism: the Disciplined Pursuit of Less*. New York: Crown Business.

9. "City upon a Hill." Wikipedia. Accessed February 20, 2020. https://en.wikipedia.org/wiki/City_upon_a_Hill.

10. Address of President-Elect John F. Kennedy Delivered to a Joint Convention of the General Court of the Commonwealth of Massachusetts, The State House, Boston. January 9, 1961.

11. Ronald Reagan. 1989. Farewell Address to the Nation. January 11, 1989.

12. "Brooklyn Historical Society." Brooklyn Historical Society. Accessed February 7, 2020. https://www.brooklynhistory.org/.

13. "Muslims in Brooklyn." Brooklyn Historical Society. Accessed February 7, 2020. https://www.brooklynhistory.org/projects/muslims-in-brooklyn/.

14. Reagan. 1989. Farewell Address.

15. Collins, Jim. 2001. *Good to Great: Why Some Companies Make the Leap and Others Don't*. New York: HarperCollins.

16. Baldwin, Joan. 2019. "Museum Staff: An Investment Whose Protection Is Overdue." Leadership Matters (blog), December 2, 2019. https://leadershipmatters1213.wordpress.com/2019/12/02/museum-staff-an-investment-whose-protection-is-overdue/.

17. Manville, Brook. 2018. "To Renew Our Democracy, Get Back To The Core." *Forbes*, January 3, 2018. https://www.forbes.com/sites/brookmanville/2018/01/02/to-renew-our-democracy-get-back-to-the-core/.

18. Quoted from an email correspondence between Vivian Zoe and the author.

19. Quoted from an email correspondence between Ruth Haus and the author.

20. Quoted from an email correspondence between Susan Edwards and the author.

21. Quoted from an email correspondence between professionals at the Monterey Bay Aquarium and the author.

22. Weil. 2004. *Rethinking the Museum*, 46.

23. Gurian. 2007. *Civilizing the Museum*.

24. Weil. 2004. *Rethinking the Museum*, 56.

25. Ronald Reagan Presidential Foundation and Institute. 2020. "Medal of Honor Forum." YouTube video, 1:11:32. February 5, 2020. https://youtu.be/uYMsu81Q5vI.

Postscript

On March 5, 2020, I submitted a complete draft of this book to my editor, Charles Harmon, and let him know that I was heading off to attend the California Association of Museums annual conference. I let him know that, because of the conference, I might be slow to respond to email for the next few days. A few days earlier, on March 1, the United States had confirmed its second death from the coronavirus, in Washington State. At roughly the same time I submitted my manuscript, New Jersey reported its first two confirmed cases of the coronavirus. Though the virus was dominating the news and apprehension was growing across the country, there were no face masks, there was no social distancing, and the conference sessions went on as planned. It has now been slightly more than three months since then. The world is not the same.

On March 9, Rudy Gobert, professional basketball player for the NBA's Utah Jazz, joked about the coronavirus and touched every microphone and recorder in front of him as he left an interview podium. On March 11, he was diagnosed with the coronavirus. The game he was about to play in was canceled right before tip-off, and commissioner Adam Silver pressed pause indefinitely on the NBA season. By Friday, March 13, the virus was declared a state of national emergency. Schools, museums, restaurants . . . everything shut down. At first it was for a couple of weeks. The weeks turned into months. Our homes became everything—the office, the schoolhouse, the gym, and the restaurant. Like a record skipping during an earthquake, everything changed. Everything.

At the time of this writing, September 2020, museums in some parts of the country have reopened. In other parts of the country, they remain closed with no definite timeline for reopening. Many, faced with the dual challenge of no ticket revenue and decreased support for individuals and foundations, have furloughed or laid off sizable portions of the same frontline staff that works so closely with their community. Museum educators, as ever, have proven to be resilient, flexible, and innovative in finding ways to connect with students and the public digitally—offering programs, resources, videos, and more. Schools, also experimenting with the new normal, have assigned virtual field trips, and are linking to the collections of museums online. There's a lot of remarkable work happening, but replacing immersive, place-based experiences and programs with Zoom . . . well, it's just not the same. Trying to build community when the world has turned into a dystopian version of *The Boy in the Plastic Bubble* is not easy work.

As of September 2020, the Johns Hopkins University coronavirus map shows that there are more than 6.6 million confirmed cases of infection in the United States. Thus far, nearly 200,000 Americans have died. There are several vaccines that are in Stage 3 trials, but no definitive timeline for, well, just about anything. As I reach out to schools, districts, teachers, and community partners to see if they have any idea what the next year will look like, the answer, pretty much universally is, "We have no idea." Thus, we float through the indefinite present like astronauts untethered.

The political and economic impacts have been significant. Millions of Americans have lost their jobs and are eager to get back to work. States and counties are loosening the restrictions related to the virus even as data seems to indicate that many parts of the country are seeing a surge in infections. People are anxious to return to normal, but the evidence suggests that our definition of "normal" will have to adapt.

Meanwhile, on May 25, 2020, Minneapolis police arrested a Black man named George Floyd on suspicion of using a counterfeit $20 bill at a grocery store. One of the police officers pressed his knee to Floyd's neck for nearly nine minutes. Despite Floyd pleading that he couldn't breathe and pleas from Floyd calling for his deceased mother, the officer persisted. Floyd died. The officer has been charged with second-degree murder. The other three attending officers, who did nothing to intervene, have been charged as accessories. Floyd's death at the hands of police was not an anomaly. He was the most recent in a long history of Black people who were killed by police. That list includes Breonna Taylor, Philando Castile, Alton Sterling, Freddie Gray, Tamir Rice, Eric Garner, Michael Brown, and the list goes on and on back over the course of hundreds of years.

In the weeks since Floyd's death, millions of people from around the globe have organized, marched, and taken to the streets in support of Black Lives Matter. Though there are many museums, museum professionals, activists, and organizers who have been working on issues of race and racism for decades, this is different. As Lori Fogarty, director and CEO of the Oakland Museum of California, said, "I think this is the defining time, the defining moment of our lives as a country, as individuals and as museum professionals, let us not miss this moment. Let us not miss this moment."[1]

During their virtual annual conference, the American Alliance of Museums added a last-minute panel to address "Racism, Unrest, and the Role of the Museum Field" featuring Dr. Johnnetta B. Cole, Lonnie G. Bunch III, and Lori Fogarty.

Dr. Cole, who moderated the session, posed this question, "As museum directors: How should we respond to these crises that are haunting our country, and indeed our world, and what could and should be our role as museum professionals in the struggle against systemic racism?"

Lonnie G. Bunch III, fourteenth secretary of the Smithsonian and former director of the National Museum of African American History and Culture, responded, "I wish I could say to you this was a unique moment. On the one hand, it is because we have a dual pandemic: we've got illness and we've got racism. But on the other hand, the notion of the kinds of deaths that we're seeing and the protest we're seeing is not new. I am struck by the words of Ella Baker, who was crucially important in creating the Student Nonviolent Coordinating Committee during the civil rights movement, and when she said, 'Until this country views the death of a Black mother's son as important as the death of a white mother's son, we who believe in freedom shall not rest.'"

He continued, "It seems to me that what we're really struggling with is to recognize that at some point a country needs to confront itself. Not a people, but a country, and that in essence, what I think this tells us more than anything else is that this is a national dilemma and I want to see all Americans realize that they are only going to be made better when we grapple effectively with issues of race and racial violence."

We are in a moment. Somehow, in 2020, fate has dealt the world, the country, and our field a hand that includes elements of the 1918 Spanish flu pandemic, the Great Depression (or at least the Recession of 2008), the civil rights movement, and a bitter, toxic partisanship that has divided our country in hateful ways that conjure memories of the rift between the North and the South that led to the Civil War. Our country has lost faith in its institutions, in those elected to serve us, in our neighbors, and often in those who look, sound, or believe differently than we do. The sheer volume of historically significant issues that we now face is, quite simply, overwhelming. Tackling any one of these effectively can require years, decades, even centuries of coordinated effort.

While it is not possible for museums to solve these problems, they must be a part of working toward the solutions. They are, as institutions that exist to create a public benefit, obligated to leverage their resources—capital, cultural, and human—to that end. We must exhaust every effort and enlist museum professionals to "work hard on work worth doing." Though we've been knocked down as a country and as a field, we haven't been knocked out. I don't think that I can express what this moment means to our field better than Secretary Bunch, so I'll leave you, and end this book, in his capable hands:

> I've lived my whole career banging on the door of museums, asking museums to do better. And by that I mean helping museums understand that we need to be excellent in the traditional ways—wonderful exhibitions, build those collections, make sure we think creatively about what education really means—but we also have to be excellent in ways that matter, that changes a mindset to say, it's not enough to be a good museum. What's key is that you have to be an institution who recognizes in everything you do that the goal is, yes, I want to do good exhibitions. Yes, I want to do good scientific research. Yes, I want the kids to come to the zoo. But the reality is what you really want is you want to change and make your community, make your region, make your country better.
>
> In other words, what I want to hear from museums in their vision statements is about the greater good and that greater good is more than serving audiences, it's about helping a country find truth, find insight, find nuance, and in many ways, what I hope that cultural institutions like this can do is that they're better suited than most to define reality and to give hope.[2]

NOTES

1. Quoted from Lori Fogarty at the California Association of Museums annual conference, March 5, 2020.

2. Quoted from Lonnie G. Bunch III at the California Association of Museums annual conference, March 5, 2020.

Index

About the Author

Anthony Pennay is the chief learning officer for the Ronald Reagan Presidential Foundation and Institute, located onsite at the Ronald Reagan Presidential Library and Museum in Simi Valley, California. Each year, the Reagan Foundation works with more than forty thousand students and two thousand teachers through field trips, programs, retreats, summer camps, internships, scholarships, and university credit. The mission in their education work is to "cultivate the next generation of citizen-leaders." Over the course of the past eight years, we have served more than three hundred thousand students, more than fifteen thousand educators, and awarded more than $6 million dollars in scholarships.

The foundation's education programs have earned awards from the California Association of Museums and the American Alliance of Museums. Student alumni have started clubs and nonprofits, earned hundreds of thousands of dollars in scholarships, and been selected to moderate a conversation with former secretaries of education Arne Duncan and John King Jr. Their partnership with a local school, the Citizen Scholar Institute, has led to our partners winning the California Civic Learning Award twice, and two of the teachers being selected as Co-Secondary Social Studies Teachers of the Year by the California Council for the Social Studies.

Pennay has served as the chair of EdCom for the American Alliance of Museums, and the chair of the awards committee for the National Council of the Social Studies.